Casting Norma Jeane

A Starlet Is Transformed into Marilyn Monroe

BY

JAMES GLAEG

The Woodbine Press

CHAPTER ONE

Planes and Angles

_____

At 20th Century-Fox Pictures on a Tuesday morning in July of 1946, Ben Lyon was surprised out of a daydream. He'd heard a rustle of movement in the room and looked up from his desk. There at the door stood a stunning twenty-year-old blonde who seemed to have materialized out of nowhere. She'd stepped into his office without any appointment—or at least that was the way, years afterward, Lyon would remember their first meeting. He was, at the time, the studio's director for new talent.

She looked absolutely gorgeous, he would recall. Golden hair falling down to her shoulders. A look of unusual freshness, of childlike innocence. Dressed in a beautifully cut, inexpensive cotton print dress. The executive felt he'd never before seen anyone so attractive.

He asked her to sit down by his desk. "What can I do for you?"

"I want mm—mm—" Her exquisite complexion flushed. Lyon supposed it was because she was struck, like himself, with a feeling they'd met somewhere before. But she tried again and this time completed her sentence with a slight stutter. "I want mm—more than anything to get into pictures."

Suddenly it flashed on Lyon why she looked so familiar. He slyly rejoined, "Honey, you're *in* pictures!"

For her face and figure were already fully on public display as the cover adornments for several gentlemen's magazines currently on the newsstands. What had specially caught Lyon's eye was that an unknown girl should have found her way onto three or four of these covers during the same month. He'd also been aware, on picking up one of the issues from the rack, of a certain pleasurable awakening at his pulse even though her expression on the cover had looked rather more sweet than naughty.

The two chatted about her background as a photographer's model. He carefully ascertained that she'd recently been signed for representation by talent agent Helen "Cupid" Ainsworth. She then read some lines from a sample script for him with no further signs of stuttering. Meanwhile, Ben Lyon—himself once a film actor of no small renown who sixteen years earlier had been instrumental in the discovery of Jean Harlow—studied the girl more closely. Of his conclusions he was later to say, "You can tell with some faces, the way the flesh sits on the bones, the planes and angles. They'll photograph well."

CHAPTER TWO

Looking Glass

_____

Ace makeup man Whitey Snyder had seen screen beauties of every description out of makeup before—but never one looking quite so nondescript as the twenty-year-old blonde who appeared at his makeup-room door two days later. She could have been some fresh-faced farm kid who'd just stepped off the train from Iowa or Indiana.

Snyder asked her name to make sure there hadn't been some mistake. And yes indeed, it was Norma Jeane Dougherty. So he steered her coolly toward a chair while wisecracking to himself silently, *Obviously the guys buzzing about her here and there around the lot haven't seen her yet at five o'clock in the morning!*

Nor was the supposedly stunning new blonde done with her surprises for Whitey Snyder. Once seated—and just as if he'd spoken all his unflattering thoughts out loud—she warded him off by thrusting a large black portfolio into his hands while she set about establishing herself in front of the makeup table alone. It soon became astonishingly clear that she wasn't planning to let the veteran makeup artist touch her face.

The clock overhead indicated barely an hour before the camera had to roll on her tightly scheduled screen test. Snyder saw exactly what kind of train wreck was coming, but for the moment he wisely contented himself with earning his steep paycheck while seated partway down the table paging idly through her book of clippings and magazine covers.

Meanwhile, the girl began her vital preparations by sliding one forefinger with deep concentration back and forth over the surface of the makeup table in a weaving gesture as if to block Snyder completely out of her mind. She next consumed several long moments peering critically at the prosaic face that stared back at her in the mirror. And very gradually, as her hands stirred to the complex motions of her cleansing routines, the signs of an inexorable momentum and purpose appeared, until by the time she finished laying down her makeup base, her entire body had taken on the animation of a Flemish painter in the act of preparing his master canvas. In this attitude she then probed into her bag, at length producing out of it a single, quite ordinary and well-used lipstick brush with which she proceeded to apply, from a series of small pots arranged on the table in front of her, a painstaking assortment of lines and dots and splashes of color to every part of her face.

While the girl worked, Whitey Snyder glanced from time to time with a studied carelessness across into her mirror. Reflected there, the deftness of her handstrokes forced him to admit that she was possessed of uncommon skill at his own craft. Yet notwithstanding a striking transformation gradually being wrought on her previously lackluster features, it rose to Snyder's level of competence to understand what no girl straight out of print modeling, like herself, ever understood. Which was that makeup techniques capable of working wonders in still photography were apt to be totally wrong for pictures that moved. Particularly if those pictures moved in Technicolor.

Truthfully, with time running ever shorter, Whitey Snyder was toying with the idea of allowing a disaster to happen. After all, he'd been treated with far more deference in his day by legends of the screen who'd needed him far less than did this virtual nobody seated at the mirror next to him.

But two things occurred to make him reconsider.

For one, his furtive glances in her direction had not been lost on her. She'd caught each one of them in the looking glass, meeting his eyes there for an instant and locating in them something which she then seemed to roll over and over in her mind while she continued to work. Many minutes had first to pass, but in time she decided to speak—using only a word or two to start with, and these uttered as though merely to herself, but ultimately proffering more and more of her remarks to the quietly observing Snyder until at last she was laying bare to him all of her deliberations as she manipulated the colors on her face.

Again it felt to Whitey Snyder as if the girl were reading his own crisp, professional thoughts even as they entered his mind. Behind every stroke of her lipstick brush, she had some reason for making it, which she now acknowledged to him in a thin, distracted voice tinged always with a minor note of distress. She needed the right side of her chin brought out to appear more prominent than it really was. Or she wanted the end of her nose shaded to appear less prominent. There were dozens upon dozens of crucial adjustments needing to be made, and while making them she would take cautious sidelong glances in the mirror toward Snyder, which told him instantly that she did not believe herself attractive enough for the career she was attempting.

So candid an admission, even if an unspoken one, Whitey Snyder had never encountered in these circumstances before. Joined to the plaintive timbre of her voice and to an openness—an almost blankness—about her face, it proclaimed a truthfulness of soul that fell on him like a current of fresh mountain air into the close fetid atmosphere of the show-business jungle in which he'd moved and breathed for too long, where modesty was unknown and where people devoured each other like beasts for their

pleasure. To Snyder it was enormously appealing—and not least because everything she said
was no more than correct. Of all the would-be
movie goddesses who'd ever sat in that makeup
chair, he couldn't think of one of them who
without makeup had looked quite so much like
a passive lump of clay as this twenty-year-old
with the long awkward name that tended to slip
his mind. Not, to be sure, that any reasonable
person would ever have called her downright
unattractive. Indeed, she was decently pretty,
but in a very plain and not at all impressive way.

The other revelation to unfold—while
Whitey Snyder allowed the girl to coax back his
sympathies—was what he found in turning over
the pages of her modeling portfolio. A *Family
Circle* cover there, from two or three months
back, showed her out of doors in a flowery field,
wearing a pinafore and bending over a lamb.
Captured in her childlike pose was a wondrous
freshness of springtime which was all owing,
really, to a quality about her face. Similarly, she'd

achieved covers—during this present month of July alone—on an astonishing total of four different magazines. Obviously, with names like *Click*, *Pic*, *Laff*, and *Sir*, these showed her in considerably less than a pinafore. But in each case it was toward her fresh-appearing, singularly open face that the prospective magazine buyer's eye was actually drawn. And there—to be detected only by such cognoscenti as Whitey Snyder—her cosmetic hand had been masterfully at work. Underscoring certain features, highlighting others, and suppressing or concealing a good many more. Designing a miniature landscape, as it were, worthy of the notice of an MGM, a Paramount, or a Twentieth Century-Fox.

This girl, then—the one in the photographs—was the one whom people were buzzing about in various quarters of the studio. Whereas that other girl—the one who'd stepped into his makeup room at five o'clock this morning—had resembled her not one bit.

Except that now, wonder to behold, as that same girl stood up from the table, she *did* look almost like the girl of the magazine covers. Almost, but not quite. What might be the factor still missing, Whitey Snyder could not divine. But there was one thing concerning her makeup about which he remained absolutely sure. Right now a Technicolor motion picture camera was going see her as painted up like a clown. And just maybe—Snyder finally decided as the girl hurried behind the partition to get into her waiting costume—it would be better if she learned this lesson on her own.

They appeared on the set with time to spare. Snyder presented the newcomer to Leon Shamroy, the Academy Award-winning cinematographer whom by a miracle Ben Lyon had secured to shoot her screen test. Shamroy took one look at the girl.

"What the hell is that on her face?!" he bellowed. "Did *you* do that, Whitey?"

Snyder acted as if momentarily caught speechless.

"No, *I* did it," came the girl's voice.

"We can't photograph her that way! Whitey, take this girl back in there," growled Shamroy. "Wash this damn stuff off, do her face up right, and then get her back out here!"

Within minutes Whitey Snyder was darting around her chair, solicitously shaping into her face all the very same cosmetic effects that the girl had been striving for on her own. Only to these, his swift hands were now adding the patented blending tricks which he'd perfected over his years of enhancing the Technicolor allure of stars like Betty Grable and Linda Darnell.

Meanwhile, strangely, the girl's overconfidence had not only been reduced to the degree Snyder had hoped, but it had vanished altogether. The closer her time came, and the readier she appeared for her screen test, the closer she came to the verge of panic.

CHAPTER THREE

Particles of Light

———————————

Adjusting his lights on the three phony walls of the test stage, cameraman Leon Shamroy half expected to look up and find the giant figure of Darryl F. Zanuck towering overhead, topped by a giant, squat, mustachioed, cigar-chomping face that grinned down over his giant fingers as they artfully worked everybody's strings. For what were the persons down below but puppets in Mr. Zanuck's giant puppet show?

That included Miss Betty Grable, even though right now she was off in New York having the time of her life while under suspension from the studio for refusing to play the off-beat role of Sophie in Zanuck's dark *The Razor's Edge*. But Zanuck was still pulling Betty's strings. He knew her gambling habits exactly, and he knew that in two to three months he would have Hollywood's highest-paid star right back on the payroll just in time to start work on *Mother Wore Tights*.

Meanwhile, that's what screen tests like this one were all about. There always had to be some blonde waiting in the wings to keep Grable guessing.

A commotion rose nearby as the latest blonde reemerged from the dressing room, properly made up for Technicolor at last. Shamroy turned to look. Teetering on spiked heels while lifting up the hem of her floor-length gown, the girl had managed to trip over a mass of huge electrical cables snaking across her path and had nearly gone sprawling across the floor. Cameraman Shamroy went back to his work on the lights reasonably sure that Miss Dougherty represented no serious threat to Betty Grable.

Minutes later the girl reappeared to his view, flattened out in the glass eye of the camera's viewfinder. Despite a terrible case of nerves, she looked, in her solid-sequin gown, very pretty of course. Yet Shamroy took note that she was far from the paragon of glamor being touted by talent scout Ben Lyon. Her posture was less than perfect. Her profile was weak, especially on the right side. She also had an unusually shaped nose.

Mr. Lyon himself now stepped into the frame, and Shamroy, seated behind his viewfinder, practiced following with the camera as the executive began running the girl through her desired paces. The two stopped at a stool Lyon had just placed in the center of the stage. They turned and hovered over the small table next to it. Then they crossed to a window off to the right. The cameraman, establishing his planes of focus on the test's subject, observed that whereas Betty Grable would have been smartly hitting her marks while cracking jokes with everyone in sight, this poor girl stumbled alongside Lyon, intermittently sighing, clutching at her stomach with both arms, and emitting the beginnings of words which she appeared unable to finish. "Mm-mm-mo... Di-di-di...Buh-buh-buh..."

Miss Dougherty's dreadful case of stage fright wasn't helped by Lyon's news that the screen test as they'd originally planned it was wholly out of the question. She could forget all about the lines she'd memorized, because there was no actor here to read them with her. Nor would Mr. Lyon feed her the lines, since no sound recordist was on the job to capture them. The all-powerful Mr. Zanuck had been too frenzied with wrapping up his beloved *Razor's Edge* even to glance at Lyon's requisitions for a test. As a result, they had no budget. What vestiges of crew were present Ben Lyon had talked into virtually working on their own time. Everything—the set, the lights, the camera, even their illustrious cameraman Mr. Shamroy himself—had been wheedled and cadged at considerable effort by Mr. Lyon from the interminable tinkering still going on with Miss Grable's still unreleased *The Shocking Miss Pilgrim*.

Not that there was a single thing to worry about, Lyon assured the distraught blonde as he handed her a glittering purse into which he'd inserted a pack of cigarettes and a lighter— because of this wonderful idea he'd had.

"All I want you to do," he said, bringing his face nearer hers and trying to connect with her frightened eyes, "is to come in that door and then do what I tell you. I just want you to project yourself the very same way you've been doing in your still pictures."

He quickly strode away and called out, "Lights!" Instantly, the make-believe room became as bright as day. The cringing girl dis- appeared around a wall to take up her position offstage. Lyon nodded to Shamroy as he backed into the sidelines. Shamroy trained his camera on the door and at length signaled to Ben Lyon that he was ready. And Lyon called out, "Action!"

The door opened. Miss Dougherty took one step into the dazzling room and then paused with her hand still on the door handle. Her posture in the shimmering gown had become, unaccountably, as erect as a statue. Her breast rose and fell with excitement.

"Walk across to the stool..." coached Lyon softly.

For a second, the girl responded only by shifting her head slightly to catch a changed gradation of the light while an intriguing expression of doubt passed over her face. Then, as if irresistibly drawn to someone halfway across the room, she stepped forward with an unfolding motion of her entire body that was like the graceful step of a sleek young gazelle. Simultaneously, a smile stole into her face that grew with a sudden force until its unexpected radiance shattered every other thought that had been building in the two men's minds.

Ben Lyon glowed back at her with surprise and delight. "Now sit down…" he said in a hushed voice.

The blonde insinuated herself onto the stool in a single movement that left the sequined folds of her gown in a striking cascade over the contours of her legs while neatly exposing the extended toes of her spiked shoes.

"Take a cigarette out of your purse and light it…" continued the hushed voice of Lyon.

As she followed each of Lyon's whispered cues, it seemed that within two or three minutes' time her very physical presence had changed before the two men's amazed eyes. Her hands were steady now. All her movements were unhurried. No trace of her earlier distress could be seen anywhere in her face or body. She brimmed with confidence. And yes, thought cameraman Shamroy, she was now every bit as stunning as Ben Lyon had promised after all.

"Put the cigarette out..." continued Lyon. "Get up...Walk forward toward the camera..."

As she advanced nearer to Shamroy's view-finder, a cobalt-hued mistiness about her eyes and a garnet-hued luminosity about her lips seemed to intermingle with the scintillations of her gown. For a moment it appeared to him that millions of particles of colored light were clustering around her from all directions in a field of energy, which she in turn channeled straight into the all-consuming mechanical eye that he held trained upon her. Shamroy cocked his head above the viewfinder to better see what was happening. Perhaps, he had to conclude, it was only a freakish effect generated by a spot-light's glare on the viewfinder in combination with the glittering of her sequined gown.

But many times throughout the day, his thoughts returned to the test. He wondered intensely how it was going to turn out. And late in the afternoon, when he viewed the newly processed film on the flickering screen of the Moviola, he got a cold chill.

"This girl had something I hadn't seen since silent pictures," Leon Shamroy was to recall several years afterward of the impression it made on him. "She had a kind of fantastic beauty like Gloria Swanson. Like one of those lush stars of the silent era."

CHAPTER FOUR

Ford Sports Coupe

From a taxi rounding the corner onto Nebraska Street not many mornings later, Jim Dougherty spotted his 1935 Ford sports coupe parked in Aunt Ana's driveway. It told the twenty-five-year-old sailor that this time he'd caught his wife at home. And that so far his plan was working.

Seconds later he rang the doorbell and waited, his mind flashing down to his newly bought suit and to all the trouble he'd had finding a decent fit after docking yesterday because of wartime shortages still going on everywhere...

...When the door opened and there stood Norma Jeane.

Jim Dougherty took in a breath. She'd become a blonde. And missing now seemed to be half of the adorable chubbiness about her cheeks. Neither in body was she quite his solid old Norma Jeane, as though the shedding of the darker coloration had shifted some weight off her feet and lifted her partway up into the air.

Nor was anything else the same when their eyes met. There was no sending forth her rollicking laugh or throwing her arms up to hug him as in the wonderful days of the past. Too much had happened since then. Instead she chose to avert her look and stick out her lower lip like a sulking child.

"Why did you cut off my allowance, Jimmie?" were her first words as she drew a flimsy wrapper around herself against the chilly air. Her face was devoid of makeup. She'd come to the door straight out of bed, where obviously she hadn't been sleeping too well.

"Look, kid, you don't pay for anything unless you're getting it," replied Jim, affecting an unfeeling face.

Norma Jeane gave him a sharply pained look as if her ears had just heard something too unbelievably crass. Now here, thought Jim with delight—despite all this new blondness and sleekness—here was his same old Norma Jeane! So very proper. So easily shocked. He felt a constriction in the area of his chest and throat before the reappearing sparks of her old life and loveliness. Notwithstanding that now she had the nerve to launch into a sob story about being in the hospital in Las Vegas with a terrible mouth infection just when the government letter arrived telling her the allotment money was ending.

Jim laughed out loud as sarcastically as he could. "Well gee, Norma Jeane," he broke in,

"I'm so sorry I had that money cut off when you were sick! How thoughtless of me! Umm—I wonder, since we happen to be on the subject of surprise letters..."

This was the amazing thing, he was thinking. Here was this girl, so quick-witted and perceptive in every other way—who'd proven herself, in fact, even as far back as the day she'd married him at the age of sixteen, to be more levelheaded and adult than Jim himself had been then at the age of twenty-one. Yet at certain times, he was always having to spell out the most basic things to her.

"...I wonder," he went on, "if you maybe gave any thought to *my* feelings when you had that letter sent to me on board ship?"

Norma Jeane stared at him blankly for a moment and then just looked away. She couldn't answer.

"From a lawyer, for God's sake!" he pursued, his already-big voice growing louder. "You couldn't even have the decency to let me know in your own words that you were going to dump me!"

The booming of his voice caused her to tilt her head to one side and indicate behind her in the direction of their old bedroom. "I think my mother's getting sort of upset," she said softly.

Jim leaned inside the door to take a look. Staring up at him apprehensively from the one bed in the apartment was Norma Jeane's mother—the strange, petite Gladys who only a few months before had been released from a mental hospital. He immediately said to himself, *There go my hopes of settling everything in bed.* Which was a shame because, no matter what, everything between them always turned out perfectly in bed.

Norma Jeane seized on the distraction to start looking him over carefully while allowing a bit of the old twinkle to come into her eyes. This was a look that he loved above everything else. Never had it failed to melt his heart.

"Your suit doesn't fit," she said.

"I know. But I wanted out of that sailor suit," admitted Jim.

Saying so was tantamount to offering her a white flag of surrender after the terrific row they'd had in January. The truth of it was that since then, he'd spent most of seven months at sea in deep reflection. And now he saw that Norma Jeane—however far off the track she may have gotten in this madness of hers about modeling—had been right about something else. That purely for the sake of a little financial security in shaky times, Jim had been stretching his wartime stint with the Merchant Marine too far beyond the end of the war for the good of their marriage. It had brought her to the point where, here at the door, she was now uttering the most outlandish proposals.

"Jimmie, we can still be close," he heard Norma Jeane saying in her sweetest voice. "We can still date. We can go on just like before…" And incredibly to Jim's ears, she went on babbling about how this divorce of hers was just a career move—how she was trying to land a movie contract, how the studios only hired single girls, and so on.

"Are you crazy?!" he broke in, his mind suddenly awhirl. "I want a wife and kids. You want a divorce? We'll get a divorce! Then it's over."

"Let's talk tomorrow," suggested Norma Jeane softly. "Maybe a little later in the day, OK? Can we do it then, Jimmie? Please?"

"OK," Jim said, shoving his long arm past her and grabbing the set of keys he'd been noticing on her small table just inside the door. "I'll take the car. I'm gonna need it to get around during my leave."

"Oh!" came a little surprised cry from Norma Jeane. "Well, I really do need it to— umm…" She drew her words out, waiting for him to change his mind, because of course she wanted the car to make more of her confounded modeling rounds. But Jim had no intention of giving up the keys, and they both knew that the car was registered in his name. "...Well, all right, Jimmie."

He spun angrily around, sprang down to the walk, and strode off toward his sports coupe, finding means to congratulate himself only at the cost of wild irrelevancy, *"Good, at least I've rescued my car from her! She's a terrible driver anyway—an actual menace behind the wheel!"*

Jimmie," Norma Jeane called after him.

At the car, he turned and glowered back at her. She was standing very still in the doorway. He'd been speaking to her in a certain contemptuous tone of voice that he'd very rarely ever used before because of how deeply he knew it was capable of hurting her.

"I think...soon...I'll be making a lot mm-more mm-money," she said mysteriously.

"That's nice, Norma Jeane," sneered Jim. "I'm very glad for you."

"Bye, Jimmie," she called, her voice small. "Sorry about this mm-morning."

Even in his anger, Jim's conscience rebuked him for hurting her the way he had, but he told himself, *That's OK, she doesn't even know the meaning of hurt!* The tailspin of agonies he'd felt upon receiving her lawyer's letter aboard ship in Shanghai was rushing back on him so vividly that he choked back a sob as, without answering her, he got into the sports coupe.

Sorry about this morning! What about the divorce? What about our whole life?!

Certainly his pride had been stung by her suggesting he take a demotion from the rank of husband to that of a favorite beau while she replaced him in their bed—replaced Jim, who knew and loved her far better than anyone else in the world—with that nutty, floating-in-and-out mother Gladys whom Norma Jeane had never once gone to see in the mental hospital during the almost four years of their marriage. But worse than anything else was the aching in his heart because he hadn't even been able to embrace her this morning.

As he headed for his folks' place in Thousand Oaks, Jim took consolation in one thing. He'd been right about her so-called career. It looked no less like a failure now than it had looked to him seven months ago. Her very first words to Jim this morning about the allotment money had said it all. She was still broke. Sure, maybe she'd gotten her face on a few magazine covers around the country, but who had paid for it? *He* had! She'd emptied out their bank account. It was drained—finding that out was a big part of what had so angered him in January. She'd pawned everything except the radio. She'd even sold their silver. All this just to cover the costs of her makeup and clothes, items which were considered quite incomprehensibly by the photographers to be her responsibility. Well, if she wasn't going to be his wife, he certainly wasn't going to be her meal ticket for one more day.

But something still mystified Jim. It came to him suddenly as he drove, after he'd considered everything else, and it stopped him dead in his thoughts.

Wait a minute. Did she say she'd decided to become an actress?

An *actress?* Jim was sure he'd heard her say that. Whereas here he'd always assumed that *he* was the ham in the family, once having gone as far as to win top honors playing Shylock in a big interschool competition. It was Jim who'd rubbed elbows with the stars, having been active in the Van Nuys High School Masquers' Club with Jane Russell, who was now making a nationwide sensation in *The Outlaw*—and having been close working buddies at the Lockheed factory with Bob Mitchum, who just that past April had been up for an Academy Award for his supporting role in *The Story of G.I. Joe.* It was Jim who in the past had found occasion to introduce an overawed Norma Jeane to these old friends of his, not the other way around. So where on earth was all this coming from?—this ambition of hers, first to become a model and

now all of a sudden to act, to get into the movies? Certainly she'd never spoken a word about
the movies to him before! Not a word.

CHAPTER FIVE

Oceans of Print

————————————

"I've got it!" cried Norma Jeane several days later as she burst into her aunt Grace's home in the San Fernando Valley. "I'm an actress!"

Waving a copy of the contract in her hand, she rushed toward Grace, who stood beaming in the kitchen.

"I'm with the finest studio in the world! I'm with 20th Century-Fox! They liked my screen test! I'm really on the payroll. Look!"

But Aunt Grace, instead of reaching excitedly for the document, went to the stove for coffee while her niece gushed on about the wonderful people she was encountering at 20th Century-Fox. Not until Grace turned around again did Norma Jeane really look at her and stop. Something wasn't right. "She was still smiling at me," the younger woman would later recall, "but she was standing still. Her face was pale and she looked tired, as if life was something too heavy to carry much further."

For an instant, that sight frightened Norma Jeane. It felt as though the very foundations of her world were momentarily slipping out from underneath her. Her guardian was beginning to drink too much. This had been obvious ever since Grace's return from the four-year sojourn back east which had separated her from Norma Jeane during the war.

What a time for Aunt Grace to be falling apart! Now, just as the dream promised to turn into reality. For it had been Grace's dream to start with, not Norma Jeane's. Out of the depths of the Depression, it was Grace who'd first spoken it. From that awful hour when Norma Jeane's mother Gladys had lost her hold on reality and needed to be hospitalized, it was Gladys' best friend—Grace McKee—who had first prophesied it. They'd be standing in a long line at the Holmes Bakery waiting for their pitiful twenty-five-cent sackful of old bread, and Grace would grin down at the child who'd been left in her charge. "Don't worry, Norma Jeane," she'd repeat. "You're going to be a beautiful girl when you get big. You're going to be an important woman. You're going to be a movie star! Oh, I can feel it in my bones!"

The words had possessed the power to make the stale bread taste like cream puffs. And today, with Norma Jeane grown to half a foot taller than her pert little guardian, the dream was starting to come true.

Norma Jeane put her arms around Aunt Grace and helped her to the table.

"I'm all right," Grace protested. "The coffee will fix me up fine."

Once seated, Grace began surveying the contract's oceans of fine print. Hers had always been an absolute power of choice with regard to everything that concerned Norma Jeane. Only two things had the girl's debilitated young mother, Gladys Baker, required—that her child never be taken to live outside California, and that she never be given up to anyone else for adoption. Otherwise everything had been left up to the energetic Grace McKee, aided by a meager twenty-seven dollars a month that came from the County of Los Angeles. To feed her "niece" through all those hard years. To buy her what clothes she could. To see to her schooling. To find relatives of her own or of Norma Jeane's to house the girl during the frequent periods when it was undesirable to do so herself. To arrange at one point, unavoidably in the circumstances of the moment, for her to be placed in an excellent nearby orphanage for twenty-one months. Even to engineer a sort of interim marriage between Norma Jeane and

Jim Dougherty, when competing needs had taken Grace away to West Virginia at the start of the war.

Finally now, as legal guardian for the soon-to-be divorced but still underage Norma Jeane, it was for Grace McKee—whom marriage in the meantime had turned into Grace Goddard—to cosign her ward's contract with 20th Century-Fox.

She took up her pen and did so. The two women wept.

"I told you, honey!" cried Aunt Grace again and again, "I said you were going to be a movie star! I told you!"

"It'll be different now for all of us," promised Norma Jeane. Soon she'd buy Aunt Grace a new house, she declared, and hire her a full-time maid.

But first came the question of a name for the dazzling screen goddess-to-be whose job would be to make all these things possible. Mr. Lyon at the studio had suggested they find something better than Norma Jeane Dougherty. And immediately the new starlet and her aunt fell to discussing possibilities.

CHAPTER SIX

Five O'Clock Girls

The head of publicity for 20th Century-Fox, Harry Brand, called Jet Fore down to his office.

"Jet, this is Norma Jeane Dougherty," said Brand. "I want you to take her around and introduce her to the department."

Jet quickly sized up the new girl. His boss seemed to be singling her out for a little special treatment, and Jet was trying to gather some inkling as to why. Could she, for instance, be the girlfriend of anybody special?

"In those days," he was later to recall, "we had probably fifty or sixty girls and guys who were under what they called stock contracts. They went to school on the lot every day. Drama school, singing school, dancing school, that kind of thing. And then the studio would use them as bit players and extras in pictures. I handled all these stock kids—wrote little two- or three-page biographies on them, took them places, tried to get them little bits of publicity. Norma Jeane had been signed to a stock contract, so she was now going to be sort of under my charge. She looked eighteen or nineteen. I thought she was a pretty girl all right, but we had plenty of other girls under contract who were just as pretty. Just as pretty."

Surely, Jet presumed, she was too young to already be one of the Five O'Clock Girls. Such was the term used for a considerable troop of attractive and ambitious young employee-volunteers of both sexes known, at least at one of the studios in town, to offer unabashedly personalized services to producers and other executives in exchange for hopes of advancement in their careers. The name had been coined with an exquisite perversity to indicate not the hour at which they reported to offices all around the lot ready to perform in so questionable a way—that time actually being 4:00 p.m. sharp—but rather an hour later, when they could expect once again to be unceremoniously dumped out of the sanctums of power and back into the commonplace hallways and mean company streets.

As Jet Fore began showing the new player through Fox's Publicity offices, he pinpointed a quality about her that just might have been enough to win, on its own, the extra push from the formidable Mr. Brand. Beneath her attractive figure and pretty face began to shine a disarmingly warm personality. "She was just an awfully nice girl—*friendly*," Fore was later to remember. "I took her around and introduced

her to everyone in our big department. There
were the guys who planted our stories in the
trade papers and on the wire services. There was
our contact for the major magazines. We had
one person who only planted Louella Parsons'
column and another who only planted Hedda
Hopper's column. There was a fashion coordi-
nator, the fan magazine contact, radio planters,
and so on—about fourteen offices taking up
about a third of the administration building's
second floor. Norma Jeane charmed every one of
these people just by being a down-to-earth kid
who seemed to feel very lucky to be doing what
she was doing."

Not that, in the eyes of Jet Fore or of his colleagues, every refreshing kid necessarily had a
glowing future on the silver screen. "As a matter of fact," he would remember, "I thought
she'd probably only be around for about a year
or so."

Inevitably too, some of the others in Jet's
department were cynical enough to calculate

the odds of Norma Jeane Dougherty's ending up, during that time, as one of the Five O'Clock Girls.

CHAPTER SEVEN

Broken Cobwebs

_____

No word about the Five O'Clock Girls had ever been heard in the house on Nebraska Street. Yet there existed among Norma Jeane's closest family more than one intuitive soul who keenly sensed that the girl's new life, while admittedly thrilling, might also be fraught with perils. Consequently certain letters had passed back and forth across the country, and these, though they contained no explicit mention of the problem, had the effect of bringing Berniece Miracle to Burbank Metropolitan Airport one or two days later out of the bright summer sky.

The cleverly turned out twenty-seven-year-old, emerging with her small daughter at the top of her plane's passenger ramp, had urgent preoccupations all her own. She peered anxiously across the wind-swept tarmac at the faces of those watching the flight's arrival from Nashville, and immediately spotted that of Norma Jeane. The girl was waving one hand wildly—as Berniece was to write many years later in a meticulous recounting of the scenes of her trip—and with the other was holding strands of very blonde hair away from her eyes in the whipping wind. The two half sisters had already met once before, and their rapport on that occasion had been instant and lasting.

There was one circumstance about this particular meeting that overrode every other consideration for both sisters and made this day virtually epochal for Berniece. A technically even closer relative was expected to be waiting there with Norma Jeane. This was no less a person than Berniece's own mother, *their* mother, Gladys Baker—a woman of whom Berniece had practically no memory at all. Now the moment had come for her to put an end to years of tug-of-war between the two poles of curiosity and dread, to take her six-year-old child Mona Rae by the hand, to resolutely step down the ramp, and to meet at last the woman from whom she'd been "stolen" when she was three years old.

The nervous young mother had progressed with her child half the distance across the tarmac when she began to discern the others who were there with Norma Jeane. She recognized dear Aunt Grace bobbing on tiptoes trying to spot Berniece amidst the arriving passengers. Close to Aunt Grace stood another person clearly not Berniece's mother—a large woman with white hair who could only be the legendary Aunt Ana Lower. Ana in turn had one arm wrapped around the shoulders of a petite woman in her midforties who remained motionless and unsmiling while the rest of them all waved and beamed. This woman's hands were clasped downward in front of her body with both arms held rigidly straight. Her eyes at that moment appeared closed into slits against the wind and glare of the airfield. It seemed possible she was praying. Yet even constrained in so bizarre an attitude and at twenty or twenty-five paces away, there was a lovely symmetry to be traced in this woman's delicate features.

A sense of recognition flooded over Berniece Miracle. Here in life was the identical stamp of mysterious beauty which had comprised Berniece's only knowledge of her mother while growing up. Her father Jasper Baker—after having snatched the infant Berniece away from his ex-wife and having forbidden the woman even to be spoken of in his home—had somehow thought it proper to give his child at least a picture of her lost parent. Berniece had kept it—a small but exquisitely beautiful framed photograph—on her dresser top all through high school. Upon it she'd lavished the nimbus of her adolescent yearnings and around it built up a ponderous store of unanswered questions. What she knew factually of the maternal half of her parentage had seemed to her so pitifully insubstantial that the whole of her ancestral memory on that side of the family came to be represented in her mind by the image of a few torn cobwebs.

Norma Jeane broke away from her three companions, ran forward to embrace Berniece, and then bent down to hug Mona Rae.

"Aunt Norma Jeane, your hair is *blonde* now!" blurted out the child, correctly remembering that two years earlier, the two sisters' hair had been of an identical chestnut brown— richly highlighted with reds and ambers to be sure, but nowhere in shades so strikingly golden as this.

Norma Jeane acknowledged Mona Rae's remark by a warm flash of her eyes, but right now she had thoughts only for speeding her sister and her niece over to where the others stood. "Well, Mother, here is Berniece," announced Norma Jeane. "And this is Mona Rae."

Suddenly Berniece discovered herself to be smiling joyously. She squeezed her estranged mother's shoulders tightly while resting a cheek against her graying curls, causing the small woman finally to stir and place her arms—which till then had hung at her sides in a manner eerily like the broken cobwebs of Berniece's earlier fantasy—limply around her daughter's waist for a few seconds before bending down to give her newfound granddaughter a languid hug followed by several listless pats on the back.

Berniece's eyes gravitated toward those of Aunt Ana, the one whose letters of invitation it had been which provided the needed catalyst for Berniece to make this trip. The wise old woman, in waiting her turn to be introduced to Berniece, had not missed an uneasy expression fleeting across the newcomer's face during her embrace with Gladys. In response to it, Ana silently lifted one index finger skyward while lowering her broad, square forehead in a serene nod to give ample assurance, as the Christian Science practitioner she was, that Heaven was there to meet every felt need.

Finishing their introductions, the five women and the child then all turned, linked arms, and headed into the wind toward the baggage claim area. Meanwhile, it took little effort for Berniece to recover her hopeful smile, so likely did it seem that the tattered filaments of their shared family past were about to be transformed into something whole and lasting according to her fondest desires.

CHAPTER EIGHT

Hypnotist's Watch

"That's so ridiculous!" came a sudden and unexpected pronouncement from Gladys Baker in one of the very first weeks of Berniece Miracle's stay in Los Angeles—from which, years afterward, her memoir was to record many of the conversations that took place.

This judgment of Gladys' fell upon the younger of her two daughters—on Norma Jeane—and its effect was to totally deflate her proud and earnest work in front of Aunt Ana's hallway mirror. The girl had been attending her classes at the studio with the utmost diligence and had been bringing home exercises in drama, singing, speech, movement, and dance, which she practiced each and every day. Today it was her diction that she was improving by closely observing the reflection of her lips as she carefully rounded them to expel the classic formulation, "How—now—brown—cow?"

"You sound silly," pursued the mother, who'd stolen into Ana's upstairs apartment with some articles of clothing draped over one arm. "If you don't have anything else to do, you can come out here and help me dry-clean these."

Berniece listened from Ana's kitchen, stunned as much by the discovery of her mother's unsuspected powers of articulation as by the scathing purport of what she'd said. Gladys had scarcely spoken as many words at one time to Berniece in all the days since they and little Mona Rae had begun sharing the downstairs apartment.

"Mm-Mm-Mother," came the voice of Norma Jeane, who was only the more taken

aback, "I have to improve mm-mm-my enun-
ciation—mm-mm-my vowels..."

"Well, *I* have to improve these dirty blouses,"
retorted Gladys, "because I can't afford to pay
the dry cleaners!" She wheeled around and
headed for the back door where, this time with
much clatter, she disappeared once more down
the outside stairs.

Berniece stepped to the kitchen doorway
and looked soulfully over at her younger sister.
Norma Jeane did not move from her spot. Her
eyes only dropped to the chest below the mirror.
The expression of disheartenment on her stricken
face seemed so uncharacteristic of Norma Jeane
that Berniece felt embarrassed even to witness
it. *Well, this is terrible*, she thought. Just when
such exciting things are happening in Norma
Jeane's life! Wasn't the girl earning a more than
reasonable seventy-five dollars a week from the
studio for the very purpose of readying herself
for the future in this way? Who could have
dreamed that Gladys was not proud of her?

Berniece strode to the end of the hall and stood at the back door with one hand on her hip and her head tilted quizzically as she looked down into the yard. Gladys was, as Berniece would later remember, "seated on the stoop beside the garage, savagely sloshing a blouse in a pail of cleaning fluid."

"Mother, you ought to *encourage* Norma Jeane," Berniece called down the back stairs. "She's trying so hard to make a go of it, and you're being so ugly about it."

Gladys looked over her shoulder and muttered something back to Berniece under her breath.

"What did you say, Mother?"

"I said I don't like her business."

Now here, truly, was one for the books! was all Berniece could say to herself in wonderment. In the brief time she'd known her mother, however, she'd learned that it was no use trying to tease out more of her thoughts on the subject. Gladys would be saying nothing more about this or about anything else perhaps for the rest of the day. All she was going do was to sulk, which was what she seemed to spend most of her time doing.

Yet here was a new piece of information, come to light at a time when every tidbit of communication from her long-estranged mother felt hard-won and precious to Berniece. So Gladys didn't like the film business? Notwithstanding the fact, of course, that it was she herself who'd brought Norma Jeane into the world as the very child and offspring of the glittering movie trade! That particular part of the sketchy family story had already been known to Berniece for several years, its luridly tinged particulars having been literally among the very first facts about her missing parent ever to come to her knowledge back home in Kentucky. For Gladys Baker, upon divorcing Berniece's father at the age of twenty-one, had freely chosen to enter the film industry during the roaring twenties, as a negative cutter for a concern called Consolidated Film Industries. There she'd met up with her friend of a lifetime, Grace McKee, the pint-sized human dynamo who'd transformed Gladys into a flaming redhead and who'd initiated her into the fast, bohemian ways of the city of celluloid dreams. It was probably at Consolidated too, following a second unlucky fling at marriage, that Gladys had struck up her relationship with Norma Jeane's father. Whatever his name might have been, not even Aunt Grace seemed to know. Very possibly—or so it seemed to Berniece—Gladys herself couldn't even say which of several co-workers was the actual gentleman.

In any case now, twenty years later, their mother was barely managing to hold down a job in a downtown department store, putting tags on clothes. The work had been procured for her by the good Aunt Ana after none of Gladys' long-past movie employers had proven willing to rehire her.

Coming back down the hallway, Berniece found Norma Jeane still looking down at the chest beneath the mirror. The girl's lips, Berniece would later write, were pressed together in silence. She seemed to have retreated deeply within herself. Her forefinger, poised atop the chest, was moving from side to side over the polished surface in a rhythmical, weaving motion. It was like a hypnotist's watch swaying back and forth on its chain before his subject's spellbound eyes. Or it was as if Norma Jeane were methodically canceling out a mark left by Gladys' words upon her mind.

Berniece clearly sensed that now was not a time for the two of them to speak. They had spoken at length before about the problem of their mother. About how deeply they'd longed—separately, each sister unbeknownst to the other and for a period measuring now in years—for a time when Gladys might confer upon them some undefined but treasured thing which only a mother is able to give. But Gladys

Baker's heart, they'd had to acknowledge, was a lock to which she alone possessed the key. Only the aunts, as of yet, had on rare occasions been vouchsafed fair glimpses of what lay within this strange woman, and in vain had Berniece and Norma Jeane waited for similar moments of their own. So that now they began wondering if theirs from Gladys Baker were never to be more than these casually tossed-out verbal missiles of petulance and gloom like "That's so ridiculous!" and "I don't like her business."

"I keep telling myself that Mother will act better when she's been on the outside longer," Norma Jeane had said of the seven months she'd already spent sharing the lower apartment with Gladys—an arrangement which had come about in the first place only because of Gladys' begging to come and live with Norma Jeane after her release from the hospital. "But I still feel as if we're strangers," Norma Jeane had concluded.

Berniece had given Norma Jean a long, tight hug. And since the doctors had said it would take plenty of time, they'd agreed that for now they would remain patient.

CHAPTER NINE

House of Monroe

———————————

Sometimes, however, on Saturdays or on weekdays when Norma Jeane had time off from her work and training, the sisters jumped into the Dougherty Ford together with Mona Rae and approached the mysteries of their common parentage from an entirely different direction. For while it was true that Berniece had never in her life had a thing to do with the movie business—she and her brother Jackie having been spirited away to Kentucky by their father before that part of Gladys' adventure had ever begun—Los Angeles remained her heritage. She'd been born here and in that sense together with Norma Jeane represented the third generation of Angelinos on their mother's side of the family. Few activities during Berniece's Southern California sojourn afforded her more stimulation than exploring these roots.

One day Aunt Grace came along to act as guide. Their goal, this day, wasn't any of the giant walled enclaves wherein the precious, newly minted images of fabulous film stars had once passed daily through the carefully gloved hands of negative cutters Gladys and Grace. Nor was today's destination outside those studios' gates, where a surplus of set designers' fantasies seemed to have spilled forth into the animated streets and picturesque hillside roadways of surrounding Hollywood, making there an Alhambresque backdrop against which the two flappers had lived and laughed and loved away the halcyon days and nights of their flaming youth. No, bypassing all this, the

Dougherty sports coupe skirted bustling downtown, coursed beyond the sleepy Los Angeles River with its plethora of railroad tracks along both banks, and climbed gently upward to the comparatively ancient neighborhood of Boyle Heights.

This place possessed for them, as Berniece would later express it, "the aura of a trip in a time machine." Dissolved before their eyes was the present-day fastness of synagogues and delicatessens beloved for more than a generation by Jewish folk arriving in successive waves from New York and eastern Europe. Instead, in imagination, the occupants of the Dougherty Ford peered deeper into the past, at a wholly different era closer to the turn of the twentieth century. They fixed on that charmed time before the astonishing rise of automobiles had revolutionized everything. When Southern California's movers and shakers had still inhabited the fashionable Queen Anne mansions dotting all this higher ground just a quick

trolley ride from their power bases of downtown. When in identical pattern, all these same
streets had still comprised a booming preserve
for the heirs, culturally if not literally, of the
Yankee tradesmen and lawyers and real estate
brokers who'd first bargained the happily situ-
ated little pueblo of Los Angeles out of Mexican
hands.

Into this earlier Boyle Heights, the two
sisters learned, Otis Monroe had fit reasonably well—Otis having been their grandfather,
Gladys' father. Aunt Grace had told each of them
before about certain papers she held as Gladys'
conservator, showing exactly how Otis Monroe
was descended from no less a family than that
of James Monroe of Virginia, the chestnut-
haired fifth president of the United States. Not
that in the sandy-haired Otis' own brief life,
with its swift and calamitous end, there was
to be found anything to outwardly match the
status of such a vaunted ancestry. But inwardly
he'd evinced one trait suggestive of something

of that exalted kind. Otis Monroe had once *dreame*d with exceptionally bold freedom.

He'd aspired to the world of high art. He would soon be studying painting in Europe— so he'd confidently told Della Hogan, whom he'd courted in Missouri upon appearing there rather mysteriously out of Indiana while in his midthirties. Then perhaps the two of them might unmoor themselves from all the pestilent restrictions of time and space by floating down the River Seine in a houseboat, while Otis executed watercolors of the French countryside which might well be the securing of his artistic reputation. There was, he'd told the rapt Della, the whole of the Old World to see and to portray in landscapes perhaps rivaling those of the glorious Cézanne. Then, aboard steamships, they'd circle the rest of the globe while he added luster to his creative standing via depictions of Earth's farthest and most exotic climes. For if any of the details along his life's planned trajectory had been left fuzzy, Otis Monroe had made its end point crystal clear. Here was a man destined to be respected, to be looked up to for as long as he lived, and to be remembered long after he was gone.

Della Hogan had been powerfully swayed. As much by the fine cut of his manly frame as by what she called his "wanderlust charm." Never mind that Otis was ten years her senior and was still earning his survival by digging postholes, patching roofs, and painting houses. His genteel appearance while at his leisure spoke for itself. He was "neat as a pin," she would later write, "always turned out like a gentleman—or at least a gentleman's gentleman." Furthermore, adorning the fair complexion of his left cheek was a large scar that added a dashing final touch to the robust, worldly appearance he made. This expressive mark, though actually received in a bad fall, accorded perfectly with Della's romantic notion of Otis Monroe as man well acquainted with danger.

The projected foreign adventures had seemed about to get underway when Otis went to work for the Mexican National Railway soon after they were married. But the squalid conditions they encountered in Mexico had soon propelled them back across the border and westward to the burgeoning new El Dorado called Los Angeles, where he'd found a similar job with the Pacific Electric Railway. Thus had it happened that the rest of Otis' life, instead of being about steamships plying the bright blue waters of the world, had turned out to be about train cars clanging over the parched desert clays of Southern California. His working hours, instead of climaxing in luminous flights of pigment from palette to canvas amid throes of solitary inspiration, had devolved into a sloshing on of bucketfuls of paint alongside whole crews of laboring men. And his advancement in the world, instead of bathing his small family in the perquisites and possessions of an onrushing fame, had amounted to a slogging climb from the obscurity of rented rooms to that of rented flats and then of rented houses.

Within a few years, Otis Monroe had stopped mentioning his vast artistic dreams altogether. Whether or not he still cherished them, Della did not know. That had been the worst part of it for her—the rest wouldn't even have mattered, but she'd never really come to *know* her husband. Yes, she could still, after six or seven years, look into his hazel eyes and truthfully say she still loved him. And despite his frequent drinking bouts, she still considered him to be a good man. But marriage to Otis Monroe, she wrote, was "like living with a shadow of someone." His mind and his heart had never become any more accessible to her than if he'd been the sole inhabitant of some distant planet's icy moon.

Barely had a job promotion come along allowing the Monroes to purchase their own home in still-fashionable Boyle Heights, when Otis had been seized by a horrifying illness.

Both physical and mental in nature, it was ascribed within the family to "paint poisoning." The astonishingly abrupt decline which ensued had turned him into someone in whom Della could no longer recognize anything of the man she'd married. And at the age of forty-three, Otis Elmer Monroe had died in the Patton State Hospital a howling madman.

That had been in 1909. Strangely now, thirty-seven years later in the late summer of 1946— and perhaps this was all in Aunt Grace's way of presenting the story—the appalling details of Otis' demise slipped with wonderful ease into the background. And it was as if the artist perpetually out of reach to Della were finally speaking out across the generations to Berniece and Norma Jeane. That he should choose to do so through a certain house on Folsom Street was the whimsical part of the matter, since it was the property around the corner at 2440 Boulder Street that he and Della had actually bought and owned. Exactly how the Folsom Street place had once fit into the family's scheme of things was now forgotten, except for one fact which Berniece was later to record. Here, she would write, stood "a house built piece by piece" by their grandfather Otis Monroe. Gazing upon it, they felt as if in some mysterious way this particular dwelling, lavished upon in such a variety of crafts at the hands of this one man alone, had been waiting all these years to be seen and appreciated by this one small audience alone.

The group in the Dougherty Ford saw much else on their day's excursion. Enough, in the tracing of Gladys Monroe Baker's life from those shaky beginnings, for Berniece and Norma Jeane to be assured above all that their mother had not always been what she was now. That once Gladys' most precious dream had been to bring her three children together into the home they deserved. So that in her bed that night Berniece Baker Miracle, for one, could extract nothing but hope and promise from all she'd seen and learned on this eventful day. Didn't it mean that some tiny portion of Gladys' dream was coming true at last? For although their brother Jackie was gone—long dead—here all the rest of them were, safely together. Berniece and her child Mona Rae sharing Aunt Ana's downstairs room with Gladys. And Norma Jeane upstairs with Aunt Ana. Didn't this day go to show that the ancestral stock once planted by Otis Monroe in Los Angeles—the living and breathing House of Monroe as it were—was not vanquished and gone but was still substantial and thriving under the good Ana's roof on Nebraska Street in Sawtelle? Along with one of Otis Monroe's landscape oils which still hung over the couch in Ana's living room upstairs!

No, there had been nothing about today to blemish Berniece's hopes. Rather, she'd found it rich with family legacy. So rich, she would later record, that it overflowed into her night's dreams.

CHAPTER TEN

Carole Lind

_____

For Norma Jeane's part, the stirrings of the day had had everything to do with a riddle still vexing her at the studio. The thought occurred to her now of applying to the sprightly minds of her new acquaintances in the Publicity Department for help in finding a solution. "The casting directors want me to change my name," she was soon telling three of them. "They don't like *Norma Jeane Dougherty*."

In publicist Jet Fore's workday, being interrupted by Norma Jeane was coming to be no rare thing. "I shared an office at Fox with two other guys," he would later remember. "We were the 'planters' who handled the main contacts between the studio and the press. Sort of the hub of the department. So Norma Jeane would come in there all the time—every day. Often she'd be wearing this low-cut, polka-dot dress, and she'd bend over our desks on purpose with those beautiful breasts of hers. Sure, she was selling herself, so to speak. And it was a great sell." The three men, in fact, couldn't bring themselves to take her to task for consuming too much of their valuable time.

As to her name, Jet Fore agreed with the folks downstairs in Casting. *Norma Jeane* made her sound too much like some kid fresh off the farm back in Indiana. The man in charge of new talent, Ben Lyon, had already dreamed up a more professional-sounding designation for her: *Carole Lind*. But they'd been trying this out, and the consensus was that something about this new name too still missed the mark.

"Do you have any ideas?" Jet Fore now asked Norma Jeane.

"Well," she essayed in a sweetly hesitant tone, "my grandfather Monroe was related to the president—James Monroe. I'd like to keep that for a last name, and they sort of like it downstairs. But now they want me to come up with a first name."

Wheels started churning inside the publicity men's heads. One of the three, Hugh Harrison, was muttering, "Hmmm, lemme see, uh—" when in a flash he struck upon a near rhyme with *Carole Lind*. "*Marilyn!* How about *Marilyn* Monroe?"

Norma Jeane went suddenly still. "Oh, I like that." She paused over it another instant before saying again, "I like that!"

Immediately, as Jet Fore would remember, Norma Jeane took the idea downstairs to Casting. In about an hour she came back, her mood exhilarated. "Hey, they loved it!" she told the three. "They thought it was great."

"She liked it herself," Jet would add. "It was catchy. *Marilyn Monroe.*"

CHAPTER ELEVEN

Sacred Space

To Aunt Grace too, Norma Jeane came directly with the heretofore-missing piece of the puzzle.

"*Marilyn*," pronounced Grace in her piping voice. The choice made here had to be the absolutely correct one. A world depended on it. Yet the small woman hardly paused before reacting, "That's a nice first name."

Merely voicing its three sprightly syllables produced an effect of catapulting Grace's mind forward and setting her aglow with an idea for a last name. As for the one already being discussed at the studio, it hadn't been mentioned yet by Norma Jeane, who was later to write, "I tried the name out in my mind, but kept silent. My aunt was smiling at me. I felt she knew what I was thinking."

At last Grace spoke for both of them. "It fits with your mother's maiden name."

Norma Jeane pretended to consider the idea for the first time.

Grace rolled the full name over her tongue. *"Marilyn Monroe.* That sounds real pretty."

"Well, I don't know," hesitated Norma Jeane.

"Why *not* use Monroe?!" insisted Grace. "It would make your mother so proud."

Bursting into laughter, Norma Jeane fairly shouted to Aunt Grace, "I thought so too! It's a wonderful name!" Grace also began laughing, and the two hugged.

So this was the glorious step. *Marilyn Monroe.* It was a little like the moment of magic in a photographer's darkroom when a long-sought-after image stirs to breathtaking life in the tray of developing fluid where there'd only been a rectangle of white paper before. Likewise, here was a magnificent name to fill what for so long had been only an impenetrable empty space. Never in her life in fact had Norma Jeane really had a surname of her own. At different stages she'd been called by the names of Gladys' two former husbands, but neither Jasper Baker nor Edward Mortensen was legally her father. Even Jim Dougherty's name, Norma Jeane felt, would very soon no longer really be hers when their divorce became final. It was one of those things—and there had been many of them—that she'd always had to wait for. How many times had she and Aunt Grace verged on the matter in their conversation but lacked for any actual name to say? In the forecourt of Grauman's Chinese Theater, for instance, ever since Norma Jeane had been eight years old. Whenever they'd "pay their respects," as Grace

put it, by touching the imprints left in the con-
crete by the delicate hands and tiny high heels
of Jean Harlow. Over Norma Jeane's shoulder
Aunt Grace would be whispering, "Someday
it'll be *you* putting your handprints and foot-
prints in the cement. Do you know that? Can
you *believe* that in the way that I can see it happening?" Surrounding Jean Harlow's square of
cement would be those of all the other great
stars about whom Grace overflowed with stories culled largely from the fan magazines
she devoured. Mary Pickford and Douglas
Fairbanks. Norma Talmadge. Charlie Chaplin.
Fay Wray. Gloria Swanson. Each of whom on
some brilliant past occasion had adorned his
or her sacred space with the final flourish of a
unique and personal signature. That someday
Norma Jeane would take her place among these
shining immortals was one of the few certainties
of the child's life. But precisely what the name
would be that she'd inscribe there in the wet

cement had always—being unknown—needed
to be left unspoken.

Until now. "Now I'm Marilyn Monroe!"

"That's my girl!" cheered Aunt Grace.

CHAPTER TWELVE

Cat and Mouse

_____

Breathlessly one of the next mornings, Norma Jeane swept up to the studio gate and distracted the guard by stopping to fish out her pass while Berniece strode straight onto the lot without one.

"Hurry up or we'll be late," called Berniece over her shoulder. "They're going to be furious with me!"

Quite well done! thought Norma Jeane at her sister's handling of the little ruse, which had required some careful coaching from herself. More and more her eyes were opening to Berniece's possibilities as a sister, an ally, and a friend.

The game was a slightly different one an hour or two later when she introduced Berniece to Ben Lyon, who cordially invited them to take seats by his desk. Norma Jeane had prepared her sister for this encounter too, albeit not so explicitly.

"Norma Jeane—" commenced Berniece nervously before quickly correcting herself, "—*Marilyn*—has been telling me how you helped her decide on her screen name."

The words had a slightly rehearsed ring which the suave Mr. Lyon allowed to hang in the air for a telling second before he indulged in a knowing private glance toward Norma Jeane that said, *Let's not get ahead of ourselves here, sweetheart.*

At this look Norma Jeane felt instantly crestfallen. Not that she's wasn't aware that the studio—in other words that Mr. Lyon as director of new talent—had every bit as much say-so as she herself did in the picking of her new professional name. If for that reason alone, she'd been quite prepared to tread softly with the executive whose brainchild in this process had been the less than thrilling appellation of *Carole Lind*. However, several days ago Lyon had appeared nothing less than delighted when in her excitement she'd brought him the name of *Marilyn Monroe*. As a result she'd dared hope the question was now all settled. Of course it was no use simply asking him if it were settled. She'd tried that, only to have him study her strangely and not answer. For 20th Century-Fox Pictures, she'd found, was just an exaggerated version of every other human community she'd ever dealt with since childhood. You could never be direct, honest, and clear with people. That only caused them to misunderstand. You had to speak in sign language. To communicate in riddles. To read people's lips. You had to bring your sister into the studio and hope to stumble on the truth of the matter secondhand.

Her mind returned to Berniece sitting next to her, waiting uneasily for Mr. Lyon to pick up the thread of conversation she'd opened. Clearly, Norma Jeane observed, Berniece was impressed by the man she saw. Lyon, in his midforties now, was no longer quite the household name he'd once been as an actor, yet certainly there were millions across the land who like Berniece and Norma Jeane still remembered him well. His screen romps over several decades had been opposite leading ladies ranging all the way from Pola Negri to Gloria Swanson to both of the Bennett sisters, Constance and Joan, not to mention Claudette Colbert and Jean Harlow. Therefore, when Lyon finally spoke, the deep resonance of his voice had—as specially modulated for the benefit of Norma Jeane's sister from the hinterlands— both a pleasing familiarity and an authority conferred by fame that made it not unlike that of a god speaking down from Mount Olympus.

"You two have very interesting resemblances," he said.

Lyon, in keeping with the charm for which he was famous, had hit on an icebreaker ideally calculated to pierce through Norma Jeane's preoccupation of mind. At home the sisters had minutely examined their faces for every trait they held in common and which therefore could be traced to the Monroe side of the family. Now Norma Jeane and Berniece lost themselves in showing the executive their respective hairlines, featuring luxuriant strands that waved off the foreheads of each from an identically prominent widow's peak. Next they compared for him their distinctively pretty mouths, each of which mirrored the other one's perfectly, down to their large, exceptionally white front teeth which came to just a pleasing tad short of being protruding. However, as Lyon ushered their conversation forward, Norma Jeane began to feel him exercising a subtle discrimination between his two visitors. Toward Berniece he was cordial and forthright, pronouncing himself intrigued by her married name, Miracle—to which Berniece rejoined that it was more common in parts of Kentucky than Smith, although always with the first syllable pronounced so as to rhyme with "fire." But when on the other hand their attention turned to Norma Jeane, Lyon spoke not to her but still to Berniece. He was pleased, he told her, with how well Norma Jeane had been settling into her classes and training. "Right now Marilyn is very *cooperative*," Lyon said, giving that word a cryptic emphasis, "but one day she'll probably become like most other movie queens—demanding." And at the phrase "movie queens," he laughed with what Norma Jeane took to be a faint note of disdain.

By no means of course had Norma Jeane missed Mr. Lyon's use of the name *Marilyn*. Berniece too had glanced over at her upon hearing it, for it seemed to indicate that the studio was at least going along with the first name passionately favored by Norma Jeane. Nor was there any doubt that in voicing that name, Lyon was conceding to her something of value—but only in a kind of barter, as it were, for in the same breath he took something else away. Berniece wouldn't have noticed this, being unaware of the significance held by the word "cooperative" for insiders at 20th Century-Fox. As Lyon said the word, his eyes had smoldered secretly at Norma Jeane as if to say, *I'm the man who pulled out of you a crackerjack of a screen test, and now I want to become much more to you than merely Fox's point man with respect to your screen name.*

Or so, at least, it had appeared to Norma Jeane.

Until getting that look from Lyon, she'd felt reasonably resolved that any small and perfectly meaningless intimacy that may already have passed between the two of them was not going to be enlarged upon. Certainly the last thing in the world she ever intended to become was a Five O'Clock Girl.

In this fashion, Ben Lyon—even as he cour-
teously chatted with Berniece—kept his sub-
duing glance on Norma Jeane until at last he'd
found his own roundabout and teasing way back
to the subject originally broached by Berniece
on her sister's behalf.

He was aware, he explained to her, that
Marilyn already had two names taken from the
screen, since her mother had obviously named her
after Norma Talmadge and Jean Harlow. But now
he wanted her to have a shorter and more glamorous name than *Norma Jeane Dougherty*. Something
both catchy and fitting. Several months earlier,
her modeling agent Miss Snively had hit on the
idea of turning her two first names around and
calling her *Jean Norman*. From there Lyon had
altered it to *Clare Norman*, which before many
days had metamorphosed into *Carole Lind*—the
presageful designation in which Hugh Harrison
had heard his inspired rhyme of *Marilyn*.

Lyon glanced impishly from Berniece over
to Norma Jeane. "Marilyn likes the sound of

Adair," he announced abruptly. "She wanted to be *Jean Adair*."

Berniece turned with surprise to Norma Jeane, who merely softened her face into a complaisant smile to convey to them both that the matter of *Jean Adair* now seemed to her a thousand years rather than just a couple of weeks in the past.

Thought Norma Jeane, *Better for me now to say not one word more, but only to read lips. Only to interpret sign language.* Nonetheless she felt that at this perfect juncture her sister must inevitably flash on their maternal surname and speak it out loud, so bursting with new flair and meaning had it become for both of them ever since their trip with Aunt Grace to Boyle Heights.

However, it was left for Ben Lyon to utter the momentous word.

"—But perhaps we'll use *Monroe*," he said with another of his glances at Norma Jeane. That's a family name, and the two M's would be nice."

Not without pain, the new stock player set about reconciling her nearly intractable will to the fact that the end of *Norma Jeane Dougherty* was not yet. It was obvious Lyon hadn't started the required paperwork for *Marilyn Monroe* on its way through studio channels. He knew the name was right—of this Norma Jeane was very sure. But he was playing cat-and-mouse games with her. Men always did this. They were games Ben Lyon would never have played with her sister, sensed Norma Jeane, because he respected Berniece in a way that he didn't respect herself. And why else, really, had she tried to place Berniece between them today, if not to shelter herself behind that respect? Berniece had had, all her life, a father to look out for her. That circumstance had equipped her with a certain backbone that anyone could see, even as Berniece simply sat in a chair talking and listening. She had reserves of confidence that clothed her no matter how shy and uncertain she might happen to feel at a given moment. Whereas Norma

Jeane went naked in the world. She was forever doomed to cast every man she encountered as her provider and protector. This was her terrible need. She could find no control over it. And it showed. It opened her up to these stultifying games men were forever playing.

CHAPTER THIRTEEN

Celluloid Kingdom

———————————

The sisters lunched that day at the studio's Café de Paris. Norma Jeane then hurried off to a class, and the commissary quickly emptied of its large midday crowd, leaving Berniece demurely studying her stenographic notebook like the conscientious secretary she was still pretending to be.

In reality she was keeping her eye on the entranceway, just in case some exciting movie star should still walk into the enormous room of tables where she sat alone. Cornel Wilde, it was said, was hard at work on one of the nearby sound stages, shooting scenes for a movie about horse racing to be called *The Homestretch*. Elsewhere Jeannie Crain was finishing up some last-minute work for her soon-to-be-released *Margie*. Such highly recognizable celebrities often preferred to wait for a quiet hour like this to stop by the commissary on coffee break.

Berniece, meanwhile, found her mind billowing over with images and afterthoughts of her morning which were still begging to be dealt with. Something about the totality of them mystified her. In this regard she was different from her sister, who—bless her heart—seemed to rush from one experience to another on impulse, never worrying herself very much about how any one thing happened to be connected to the next. And no doubt there was a certain wisdom in Norma Jeane's ever open and flexible ways that Berniece might do well to study and adapt to her own uses. But for the moment she longed for a chance to drop

back from the ceaseless rounds of outward phe-
nomena, to cast her eyes deeply inward, and to
find this morning's place among the forms and
shapes and patterns of the things she loved and
treasured, which were always those things that
could be counted upon to last.

Viewed on such a level, it soon occurred to
Berniece Miracle that all this curious studio
scene in front of her—taking place within a
citadel so secretive and privileged that she had
to counterfeit a look of waiting upon some particular boss's beck and call—had come to her
like a dream out of the small framed photograph on her girlhood dresser top in Pineville,
Kentucky. It completely surrounded her now,
this mysterious world which for years had lain
quiescent behind the reluctant eyes of her beautiful unknown mother in the portrait. And
which, yielding at last to Berniece's importu-
nate contemplation, had first manifested itself
by means of a wrinkled letter arriving out of
the blue from Gladys Baker herself, saying not

only that she still lived but also that Berniece had a twelve-year-old half sister called Norma Jeane. Merely recollecting that day's revelations and her own trembling reaction to them, even now over the distance of time in Fox's Café de Paris, caused the morning's images jostling for order in Berniece's mind to marshal into a magical cavalcade with those of the past.

She remembered her first sight of Norma Jeane ever on earth, which was that of an eighteen-year-old girl stepping off a train on an impulsively taken trip back east to meet her long-lost older half sister. Photographs, thus far in her young life, hadn't done her justice. Even her lovely wedding pictures with Jim Dougherty, taken a couple of years earlier, had failed to reveal anything in the plumply pretty Norma Jeane to rival the pellucid beauty of Gladys Monroe. But seen in person at the train station, how she'd stood out from all the other passengers on the platform! In part, yes, this had been due to a certain adventuresome, lithe, and elastic way she had of carrying herself in a cobalt-blue suit that nearly matched her eyes. Even more it had to do with the distinctive smile emanating from beneath the heart-shaped brim of her hat—a smile on first glance rather unassuming than otherwise, yet on second glance charged with a quality that was decisively to captivate Berniece. Which was no external attribute at all, but a sweetness radiating from *within* the girl, so subtle and penetrating as to seem not quite of this world. It was a kind of freshness that she positively exuded, like that of a rose petal unfolding in the morning dew. Little Mona Rae had sensed this characteristic no less quickly than Berniece and moreover had instinctively trusted Norma Jeane because of it. "She's pretty and sweet and soft," the child had articulated in immediate reaction to her aunt, "and she smells good, and I feel good when she hugs me."

Quite amazingly since then—reflected Berniece at her table in Fox's Café de Paris—no scintilla of this precious and exciting attribute had been obscured by the two years recently spent by Norma Jeane at so artificial-sounding an occupation as modeling. Quite the reverse: Based on her present visit to Los Angeles, Berniece was tempted to conclude that in those two years, everything else about Norma Jeane had changed and only this one thing had stayed the same!

Sometimes at Aunt Ana's, the visitor would watch in fascination while her newly golden-haired sister sat surrounded by a palette of tiny glass pots with black screw tops, masterfully wielding a lipstick brush to individually work scores of variously-hued globules of pigment onto the fine-grained and marvelously flex-ible fabric that was her complexion. Drawing a feathery line down each temple where her eye-brow hairs were too scarce to show. Defining the outer border of her mouth in deep maroon and then blending inward with ever-lighter shades of red to give her lips an illusion of glowing fullness. Darkening a colorless mole on her left cheek into a dramatic beauty spot— the delightful ghost of that dashing scar once decorating the left cheek of their grandfather Otis Monroe. And most fittingly was this so, seeing that two years at modeling had made Norma Jeane precisely what their grandfather had been before her, truly an artist with colors. She was now a highly trained professional capable of viewing herself as the sum of many flawed parts and pieces, each of which with relentless perfectionism she had to shape and alter and streamline in order for that freshness or sweetness innate within herself to outwardly shine.

Yet nothing in all these preparations of Norma Jeane's quite accounted for the results that Berniece had witnessed this morning at 20th Century-Fox.

After their meeting with the charming Ben Lyon—and using goodness only knows what wiles—Norma Jeane had managed to book a private viewing of her screen test for her sister.

Through narrow, stucco-walled outdoor passages, the two had found their way to a tiny theater normally reserved for the highest inner circles of movie production. Inside it they'd taken their places amidst several short rows of vacant seats. A weighty door to the booth at the back of the room had closed to block off the clattering hum of a massive film projector. The lights had dimmed. And noiselessly up on the big white screen had flashed the fleeting sequence of silent images which had gained for Norma Jeane her little toehold inside the celluloid kingdom.

Gazing in keen anticipation up at the screen, Berniece had seen a door open. And there in vivid color had stood Norma Jeane, encased in a tight-fitting evening gown and looking somehow sleeker and more idealized than she ever had in life, even in full makeup. The initial sight of her had struck Berniece, as the girl's own sister, with such unfamiliarity that involuntarily she'd taken in a breath. What in the world did this glossy siren have to do with the warmhearted, often plain-looking girl at home who chattered and giggled with Berniece at bedtime, her head covered in pin curls and encircled by a hairnet?

But as an avid moviegoer, Berniece had, in only seconds, become intrigued. Obviously the test role assigned to Norma Jeane by Ben Lyon was that of a young and beautiful temptress. As to what sort of place this character had entered and what it was that she seemed on the point of doing there, Berniece's curiosity hadn't yet been satisfied when the real Norma Jeane sitting next to her in the little theater had spoken up with some observation or other about her gown or makeup in the test. This one remark alone wouldn't have distracted Berniece, but Norma Jeane had then gone on to scrutinize aloud each and every move and expression made by her on-screen persona who now successively crossed the room, sat down on a chair and lit a cigarette, put it back out again, stood up and approached the camera, turned, and stepped over to a window to look out. Scarcely a minute had elapsed before the images had stopped again. When the lights had come back on, Berniece had sat slightly stunned. From a cloud of reactions buzzing about in her head, she'd endeavored to separate those belonging to Norma Jeane's analytical commentary from her own spontaneous impressions, the first of which had been of a swift pastiche of very bright pretty colors, of marvelously rich tonalities everywhere strikingly present both in the *Shocking Miss Pilgrim* set used as a background for the test and, above all, in Norma Jeane's eyes and lips and skin.

The short piece of film hadn't stopped working its effects on the wondering visitor to 20th Century-Fox when—into the Café de Paris strolled Cornel Wilde!

Instantly every pretense of Berniece's as a blasé secretary dropped away, and she simply stared at the Olympic-level ex-athlete with the curly black hair and soulfully dark piercing eyes. On

movie screens back in Kentucky and all across the
nation, Cornel Wilde this year had been proving
himself a worthy successor to Errol Flynn in the
role of the son of Robin Hood in *The Bandit of
Sherwood Forest*. Berniece had formed a compel-
ling impression of him which now tallied won-
derfully with the person moving and breathing a
few steps away from her—or rather, it tallied in
every respect except one. The actor, while perfect
in all the proportions of his handsome face and
athletic form, stood approximately a foot shorter
than she'd expected! Berniece couldn't help feeling a sharp sense of letdown. Of course a man's
height wasn't something he could control, but
neither did Berniece feel totally at fault that
in watching this player's high-energy exploits
on the screen, some part of herself had gotten
personally invested in another, different Cornel
Wilde—one who stood a foot taller than this
man now in front of her. No wonder the movie
companies built their production studios in the
tightly sequestered way they did, if secretly

behind the high walls and iron gates, all they were manufacturing was illusion!

That was the thing. Arguably Norma Jeane's screen test was no different. The apparition it showcased stood a full foot taller—in a manner of speaking—than did Berniece's real sister, even at her most groomed and glamorous. Such was the celluloid kingdom's uncanny triumph that Norma Jeane now far surpassed the beautiful woman in the small framed photograph on Berniece's girlhood dresser top. She'd become, within the otherworldly dimensions of a movie screen, suddenly luminous. Suddenly gorgeous. All her actions and even the objects surrounding her now vibrated with exciting life.

"The screen test," Berniece was to write many years later in her detailed recollection of that morning at Twentieth Century-Fox, "stayed in my mind for days."

CHAPTER FOURTEEN

Smoke in the Wind

At sunset on the evening of one of those same days, Jim Dougherty stood alone on the deck of a freighter coursing across the middle of the wide blue Pacific. His work shift was finished. Now he stood with his arms propped up on the rail, looking out over the huge ocean. It was time to face facts about Norma Jeane.

Such a rarity anymore as a letter from her—who'd once written to him gushingly every single day—had reached him at one of the ports recently. In about as few words as it would have taken her to tell him to pick up some groceries, she was informing him that their beloved dog Muggsie was dead. She'd been too consumed by her new career to take care of the poor animal and had left it to languish on Jim's mom's back porch, where no one else had paid much attention to it either. Finally the once-pampered creature had simply stopped eating and died.

The letter's curt tone, reflected upon now at ship's side in the dying rays of the sun, gave Jim all the sign and portent he needed to read his own future with regard to Norma Jeane. It was for this moment that he'd refused to sign the divorce papers during his last shore leave. Anyone then would have said he was only refusing out of frustration and spite—both of which he'd admittedly felt more than once during the afternoon they'd spent driving around the Valley revisiting their old haunts—because every time their conversation had begun to look encouraging, she'd turn it back round to, "But please, Jimmie, sign the papers." What his stratagem of not doing so had gained him, however, was the time he needed to see things clearly, the way he was seeing them now.

It was over. For the past couple of months he'd only been clutching at straws, the most recent of these straws being Norma Jeane's proposal that the two of them "stay close." That was a hope in vain, Jim now saw, since it was clear that her sudden fever to make it big in Hollywood wasn't just some bad idea put in her head by this modeling-agency woman Miss Snively as Jim had been supposing all along. It was coming straight out of Norma Jeane herself, who wanted it frantically enough to abandon poor Muggsie—not to mention their marriage—on account of it. Nor was there any hope left that these farfetched ambitions of hers might pass away with the changing winds of her many other moods. Too much time had elapsed for that now. Ill-advised though such dreams and desires notoriously were, she was actually determined to pursue them. And if there was one thing you had to say about Norma Jeane, it was that when her mind was made up about any course of action, she'd follow it through to the bitterest end.

So then, what had the whole wondrous and magical scene been four years earlier? When like a dream she'd descended the spiral staircase at the Howells' house and promised to become his wife forever. Had it all just been some big performance on her part? Jim Dougherty's keen recollection of that June evening convinced him otherwise. To be sure, there'd been an audience present, what with two dozen and more friends and relatives gathered in that borrowed home's central hall to witness the ceremony. And no doubt every single one of the guests had gotten caught up in the pristine glow cast by Norma Jeane, who at sixteen had looked like an angel in her pure white gown of embroidered lace. But with every "hesitation step" she'd taken down to the place where he stood, her shy smile had been fixed on Jim and on Jim alone. Well, then could it have been a performance meant for him and for him alone? To know differently, Jim had only to remember how it had felt once their eyes had finally left each other's and they'd both turned to face Reverend Lingenfelder. The closing notes of the wedding march played by Aunt Ana on the piano had signaled for everyone to sit down again and hear the exchanging of the vows. And as if it were happening right at this moment, Jim could still feel the presence of Norma Jeane as she had stood next to him, could still smell the very fragrance of her while they repeated those promises. How soft and sweet her voice had sounded to him as she spoke! And a little scared, for truth be told, he'd felt her whole body trembling right up to the moment when Reverend Lingenfelder had pronounced his words over them and they'd turned to look at each other again. It was right then, unexpectedly, that Norma Jeane's bright face—bordered by soft ringlets of glossy brown hair tumbling down from beneath her veil of white lace—had made one of those iconic pictures never to be erased from his mind for as long as he lived. She'd smiled up at him, and something boundless had entered into her wide blue eyes. There'd been a whole world of sweet intimations shining in that look, but above all it had said to him, "I trust you," causing Jim to stand there dazzled in his rented white tuxedo, feeling as though he'd just taken part in a miracle. Norma Jeane had entrusted him with her heart for all the rest of their lives. She, in whose beautiful eyes he'd sometimes felt he might drown, had now become his wife in full majesty of the law and in the full sight of both God and man!

No, this had been no performance on Norma Jeane's part. Of that Jim Dougherty was positive as he gazed over his freighter's rail at the broad blue sea. And more proof of it was in how happily they'd lived together afterward. Nothing beyond the predictable things, a few trivialities, had ever gone amiss between them. At least not until much later, after he'd shipped out to sea, when she'd stumbled upon this accursed obsession of hers with modeling. Only since then, only in the past year and a half had there taken place a change in her which Jim found to be nothing short of appalling. For never in the world would the modest, the often even terribly proper girl he'd married in 1942 have made the suggestion that Norma Jeane had made on the recent afternoon they'd spent driving around the Valley. She'd wanted the two of them go on living together just as before—but, in so many words, *without* being man and wife. Where on earth could she even have picked up such a notion, if not from Miss Emmeline Snively or from some other person involved with this Blue Book Modeling Agency?

No, it was over.

In the time Jim had stood at the ship's rail thinking about it, the red sun had hurried below the horizon. And for as long as the blue ocean continued to shimmer in its afterglow, he practiced setting his face away from what he now realized he'd been living on for too long— all the aching memories of those two, perhaps three years of his young life filled with a profound bliss, but a bliss so illusory as to prove capable of then disappearing as fast as smoke does in the wind.

"Finally, as it got darker," Jim Dougherty was later to write, "I felt myself sigh deeply, and I pushed myself away from the railing. That tiny gesture was an oddly freeing movement for me. I remember it so clearly. I suddenly accepted that there was no place for me in Norma Jeane's future. None in the least. She was perhaps willing to occasionally toss me some crumbs of affection, but I was not at all willing to settle for that. It was over. No more crumbs. No more straws. No more smoke. I went below."

CHAPTER FIFTEEN

Black Lace

Someone much closer to Norma Jeane than was suspected by even her family—a winsome and fast-rising personality in the world of glamor photography called André de Dienes—was at this moment right in the middle of posing ten ravishingly beautiful fashion models in New York's finest hotels and most spectacular seaside mansions for Montgomery-Ward's winter catalogue, when something inside him snapped.

Suddenly de Dienes realized he was fed up with waiting forever for bad telephone connections to Los Angeles. All he wanted to do was get in his car, drive straight to the West Coast, and marry Norma Jeane. Summarily, therefore, the photographer quit his posh assignment to the astonishment of friends and associates who concluded that the impetuous thirty-two-year-old had been driven by overwork into a nervous breakdown.

"But André," came a tortured admission from Norma Jeane over the crackling long-distance line after a struggle within herself when pressed by de Dienes to meet him in Las Vegas, "I don't want to get mm-mm-married. I want to get into the mm-mm-movies."

Six days later nonetheless, the strapping blond Transylvanian was waiting at the corner of Sunset and Vine at exactly the hour of the afternoon when Norma Jeane had promised over the phone to meet him. But Norma Jeane did not appear. He waited there for two more hours and then drove to her apartment in Santa

Monica with a certain possibility of mischief lurking in his heart.

It was a little one-room pied-à-terre she'd taken on the side—strictly a secret from the family on Nebraska Street till her Nevada divorce became final and the two of them should be free to marry. Or so at least she'd allowed the love-struck photographer to view her peculiar living arrangement. He was just parking there when, sure enough, out of her building came a nicely dressed gentleman, perhaps in his late forties, whose discreet manner immediately suggested to de Dienes that he'd been there to visit Norma Jeane. The man strode coolly over to an expensive car, got in, and drove away.

De Dienes went up to her door.

Opening unsuspectingly to his knock, Norma Jeane turned pale. She clutched a negligée more tightly around herself, precipitating glimpses of black lace sliding over the curves of her otherwise naked body which set loose in de Dienes' rattled mind the singular phantasm of a sleek young panther freshly sprung out of its cage and peering dangerously about after prey—a conceit totally at odds, however, with the stunned look on her face as sputteringly and stutteringly she tried to explain why she hadn't been there to meet him on the corner of Sunset and Vine. Either she'd forgotten or she hadn't believed he was really coming. He himself was too stunned to decipher which.

De Dienes could scarcely speak. Slamming through his head came a host of denials, *Absolutely not a hooker!* being the first of them to solidify into a distinct thought—as in his memory he flashed on how she'd appeared at his hotel door at the Garden of Allah less than a year before, a brand-new girl sent to him by Emmeline Snively. She'd worn an immaculate pink sweater, her curly brown hair tied with a ribbon to match, and checkered gray slacks. *Unsure of herself,* de Dienes had observed at once, *Awkward and young...* They'd spoken for only another minute or two before he'd further noted, *Childlike smile...Strikingly clear gaze... Particularly clean!..*For he was only too personally aware that unbeknownst to Miss Snively, a few of her Blue Book girls were hustling. *Absolutely not a whore!* he'd concluded of Norma Jeane without a shadow of a doubt. He'd been enchanted.

Now at her own apartment door, the fact of her having gone golden blonde in the meantime lent in de Dienes' eyes, if anything, a certain enhancement to that freshness and innocence foremost in his memory. His shock lay purely in what the black lace telegraphed, as reinforced by a single instant of frightened recognition fleeting across her face. She was exposed.

"I made my way into a cluttered room," de Dienes would write many years afterward of the scene before him. "Very untidy. Records, photos, and stockings lay on the floor, a crumpled dress on a chair. There were dirty glasses and an empty bottle on the table. And a bed, rumpled."

De Dienes looked for a place to sit, with Norma Jeane hovering behind him and uttering shards of confession through sniffles and tears, seemingly to the effect that the gentleman visitor she'd just entertained was someone of influence at the studio. Was she ashamed? Or was she afraid? Possibly both, the photographer surmised. Meanwhile, however—the whole project of talking her into marrying him now appearing in a garish new light—his mind was in full process of whirling like a calculating machine, adding up increments for each week and month he'd invested in creating their rapport as photographer and model…subtracting ruthlessly for his six days' drive across the country, not to mention for an anger and jealousy fully aroused in him but no longer having any useful place…multiplying by the inestimable factor of his recurring and often powerful hunch that a splendid future lay ahead for Norma Jeane…then dividing by the grave advice of peers who said that de Dienes, being infatuated, was vastly overestimating the starlet's salability and strengths.

All this arithmetic and much more he achieved in seconds, arriving at a total reliable enough to slap a wry smile on his face by the time he and Norma Jeane were seated face-to-face.

He didn't really care who the man was, he told her. After all, what kind of celebrity photographer would he be if he didn't understand the role of the casting couch in her chosen line of work? She wanted to be free? OK, she was free. In fact, he said, he didn't blame her one bit for not wanting to marry a crazy—if supremely talented—Middle European such as himself. And he'd harbor no hard feelings either—*so long as he was still her favorite photographer!*

This was all Norma Jean had wanted to hear. Soon she was laughing with him as though nothing had happened. And why, the photographer cynically asked himself, shouldn't she laugh? She'd just managed to retain her access to André de Dienes, whose mere signature was a recommendation to the editors of *Vogue*. It was he who'd recently put her on the cover of *Family Circle* and who in fact had top contacts with all the right magazines, both American and foreign.

"What do you think of this name—?" Norma Jeane soon asked him.

She picked up a pencil and tried out her signature on a notepad which he'd already spotted on her coffee table. Its open page had been covered with the same two words over and over again, each of them starting the large, swirling capital letter M.

"—*Marilyn Monroe*," she announced, holding up the notepad for him to see.

De Dienes' eyes for a second time rested thoughtfully on its handwritten flourishes.

"Well, don't you like it?" asked Norma Jeane.

"It isn't that," he responded slowly. In fact, the name sounded perfect. But momentarily he was allowing his shaken senses to take refuge in a memory undreamed of by anyone like Norma Jeane living in a world so far removed from his own childhood homeland.

For what he was hearing wasn't a movie star's name at all, but the clear sound of a bell arising from the thickness of the Turia forest and resonating outward with the message of the angel to the Virgin Mary, upon the hearing of which many of the devout among the neighboring farmers and villagers were still known to stop everything they were doing and to repeat their Angelus prayers. That serene picture made a poor match, to be sure, with the one actually before him of Norma Jeane sitting across the coffee table, naked underneath her black lace negligée. Yet spontaneously the memory of it had rushed over him as soon as he'd noticed her notepad lying there covered with the swirling M's. The sight of it had put him in mind of the white-whiskered, long-haired old bell-ringer who lived in his tower in the forest, surrounded by many curious old books among which there'd been one featuring an ornate illumination of the letters MM—for the Latin "Memento Mori," meaning "Remember that you must die."

That somber thought, joined to the intoning in his memory of Turia's ancient bell, brought to André de Dienes' mind a picture of Norma Jeane and her Aunt Ana bowing their heads in prayer at lunchtime. That fine old lady had invited André to share a meal with them before she would consent to her niece's going away with him on a month's journey to pose against a backdrop of the California wilds for his camera. It was to be her first truly professional assignment.

Subsequently on the road with André, Norma Jeane had gone right on bowing her head in prayer every time they'd stopped for a meal. All about her, no matter in what circumstances, there continued to cling a certain demure and proper air that never once verged on prudery. De Dienes had delighted in this. It underlay, he'd discovered, all her expressions of face and all her postures of body. Especially, in their work, it had added an unexpected zest to the inborn knack she had of sporting before the camera a fanny which had proven to be of uncannily compact excellence when encased in the blue jeans he'd newly purchased for her, her very first pair.

Of course the photographer had explored every part of her body in his imagination before he'd ever touched her. On one particularly hot and dusty day when he'd gotten all sweaty and frustrated trying to fix a flat tire at the road-side, he'd happened to look up and see Norma Jeane sitting at a distance on a large stone— her makeup perfect, her clothes spotless, the very picture of pristine calmness and compo-sure. He'd dropped his tire iron right then and there, and the next minute he'd been at her side thanking her for simply coming along with him and begging her to marry him! In the sur-prise of the moment she'd only turned her face away and said nothing.

Weeks later, however, after he'd grown so vilely exasperated and petulant with her stand-offishness that she'd finally submitted to his advances, he'd reveled in an experience of love exceeding all his expectations. Until morning, that is, when he'd found the twenty-year-old sobbing quietly into her pillow. It hadn't been, he'd found, what *she'd* wanted to do at all. Only something she'd allowed *him* to do. Stabbed by the feeling that he'd practically kidnapped Norma Jeane, André de Dienes immediately knew just how he would make everything right. It was a fact that he adored her. He would make her his own the minute she was free to marry!

Now as the two spoke in her little one-room pied-à-terre, the black lace negligée made it clear she'd been stringing him along about marriage all this time only because of what he could do for her career. He'd known that kind of girl—and used them—plenty of times before in Rome, Paris, New York. But finding that Norma Jeane had become one of them was a thing hardly possible for him to accept.

For some reason, when he left her at her door, their embrace felt like one between a brother and sister. About that and about everything else Norma Jeane appeared relieved, pleased with the outcome of a sticky situation.

It was only for André de Dienes to feel otherwise. Yes, he prided himself on how swiftly he'd always adapted to crises, and his sangfroid in the handling of this one had been professionally for the best. But now he was going to have to awaken like one of the white owls in the dark shadows of the Turia forest at the ringing of the Angelus bell. Now he was going to have to come to terms in his heart with his discovery that he'd been living in a dream about Norma Jeane. How was it possible to say that nothing here had been lost to him? *His dream, after all, was his dream!* Therefore, he was anything but through with this nervous breakdown his friends said he was having. He was definitely going to get drunk tonight. And very seriously he felt he might just go drive his car off a cliff and kill himself.

CHAPTER SIXTEEN

Scroll of Life

———————

Within a breathless period of barely more than a month, Norma Jeane had achieved three of her paramount goals. She'd won herself a movie contract. She'd gained the companionship of a sister. And now by mid-September, after motoring across the Mojave desert to Las Vegas with just enough time having elapsed for Jim Dougherty's formal consent no longer to be required on the legal papers, she'd obtained her Nevada divorce.

"I'm a free woman!" she exulted to Berniece upon returning to Los Angeles, "Oh, I feel like celebrating!"

Accordingly, telephone lines began buzzing in and out of the Nebraska Street house, and soon the oddly-assorted collection of souls who remained her closest family in the world joined the freshly divorced twenty-year-old at the most elegant restaurant their severely war-tested means could afford. There, not even the presence of Gladys Baker was expected to restrain the tide of jubilation sweeping round their luxuriously appointed table. For although it was old news that Gladys had tasked herself with serving as a wet blanket over her daughter's fondest hopes and dreams, thankfully the mother seldom made any great show of this in public, preferring smaller and more intimate occasions instead. She waited, perhaps, for the girl to come home in a transport of joy over some little stroke of professional success, the more deeply to sting her with a half-dozen curt words of scorn over what Gladys called her "business." Or she might chance to overhear as the girl received a phone call quoting some well-placed person in praise of her work—and afterward fix on her only a grim funereal stare. One had to presume Gladys acted from some motive loftier than that of gratuitously wounding Norma Jeane, yet it was clear that these moments fell like hammer blows on a wedge of iron irretrievably cleaving the daughter from the mother. Not even the wonder-working Aunt Ana seemed able to heal the widening breach between the two, except in keeping dear Norma Jeane's heart perfectly unembittered and her plans and ambitions not one whit less keen and alive.

So matters had stood when, shockingly, another voice was heard to speak in the same tones as Gladys' just inside the restaurant door. It belonged to no less trusted a figure than one of her uncles, Sam Knebelkamp, who immediately upon meeting up with his wife Enid in the vestibule muttered to her that any pretty young thing going into the movies was like a child playing with fire. And this from the gentle, balding Sam who'd never said a word against her career before!

Enid simply laughed. What on earth possessed Sam, she'd wondered, to say anything so ill-suited to this night's celebration?! To be sure, there was in his normally benign face an evil portent which suggested that her fine humor might be spoiled if she found out. But Enid, reckless in her access of joy, obeyed an impulse to exorcize the moment of any such prompting by parroting her husband's words with a jocund show to Doc Goddard. The inevitable result was that by the time the family were seated, some version of the Sam's jarring utterance had reached the incredulous ears of nearly everyone there—quite possibly including Norma Jeane.

Later, as the waiter cleared away the soup course, a lull in the chattering of the family's voices allowed Sam Knebelkamp to reach out and gloss over as best he could the incident at the door.

"Everything really seems to be working out the way you've hoped," he spoke up in a kindly voice to his sometime foster daughter. No one, after all, doubted that he thought the world of her, having in his day probably put in fully as many hours looking after her as Gladys Baker ever had done. "We're really happy for you, honey."

There was a soft general sigh of relief. Automatically the eyes of everyone around the massive table turned warmly upon Norma Jeane in the lively hope that with all her new training from the studio, she might deliver some witty and icebreaking response to Sam's gracious words. But no—her face wore only a certain slightly stunned expression well familiar to most of them ever since she'd been seven or eight years old. This would quickly pass, they knew, being caused only by that peculiar species of panic she'd always felt when more than a certain number of people looked at her all at one time. It was the family's custom to nudge Norma Jeane pleasantly but firmly right past these fleeting little episodes, and the girl's solicitous Aunt Enid now thought to do so by voicing the very question her husband's earlier remark had put uppermost in everyone's minds.

"No flies in the ointment, Marilyn?" she ventured, pointedly speaking out the musical first name that her niece was newly insisting the family use from now on.

At first the girl only shook her head in reply. She then found her voice and stammered out, "N-N-None!"

"What about the problem the other day with your agent?" essayed Doc Goddard, who like Sam had put in his own share of time as a foster father to Norma Jeane by virtue of his being married to the twenty-year-old's legal guardian, Aunt Grace.

Sam Knebelkamp again leaned assiduously forward. "What was that? Or am I prying?"

In reality, Sam didn't care one bit about her agent. Right now he only wanted to watch how his onetime charge was comporting herself, this in light of doubts which had been plaguing his mind all day but which he certainly hadn't intended to share with anyone here tonight except his wife. For as a man employed in a supervisory capacity by a telephone company with its tentacles reaching into every office in town including those of the movie studios, he heard things. And earlier today he'd happened upon some unsettling information—rumors from one of the studios about a thoroughly bad set known as the Five O'Clock Girls as well as about the men in power who used them. Not that Sam Knebelkamp or anyone else taking one look into Norma Jeane's innocent eyes could believe she'd ever turn into that kind of woman. What in fact bothered Sam was that she was entirely *too* innocent. She had no under-standing of the way men looked at her body, of how profoundly even its subtlest movements underneath her clothing had the power to disturb their thoughts. It was obvious, given the atmosphere in which she was working, that demands were going to be made on her. All this studio business, Sam had reluctantly become convinced, wasn't going to end well for Norma Jeane.

"Oh, it was nothing," replied Norma Jeane to his question about her agent. "I mean, it wasn't anything I shouldn't expect. He was on the phone with me, wanting an increase in his percentage, that's all."

Calmly and gravely, Sam Knebelkamp continued to listen and probe. He observed that Norma Jeane had begun pitching her voice up a notch as she went on explaining, but to Sam she sounded too full of high spirits for anything terrible or even anything very troubling to have been happening to her recently. More likely she'd simply gotten wind of what Sam had grumbled to Aunt Enid at the restaurant door.

"It was *nothing*!" emphasized Norma Jeane again of her altercation with the agent.

The bird-like voice of Aunt Grace piped up in assuagement of the concerns she clearly read on Sam Knebelkamp's face. "They got it worked out. It simply means our girl is getting more important."

This opinion caused the eyes of all the others to turn instinctively to Aunt Ana Lower as the family's ultimate seer into what any event might portend. Indeed, Sam himself gave much credence to Ana's opinion on all weighty issues, if only because of the great goodness in her which had never been known to fail. But—Sam now had to consider—in the mind of the sainted Aunt Ana, creatures like the Five O'Clock Girls did not even have existence, at least not as such, since nothing evil had for her any trace or token of reality by reason of her profound moorings in Christian Science. In that respect she could be of no more help to Norma Jeane than could any of this Atchinson family into which Sam

had married. Such had been the maiden name
of the girl's Aunts Enid and Grace, who were
sisters, as well as of Aunt Ana who was in turn
their aunt. There was about all three of these
redoubtable women a rich streak of the dreamer
that needed close monitoring—a proclivity for
fantasizing away dangers that had been anything but lost on Norma Jeane. For while it
was technically true that the Atchinson women
constituted only a surrogate family whose bond
with the girl rested solely on the inscrutable
ties of friendship between her mother and
Aunt Grace, despite the absence of any blood
ties, Norma Jeane took after these aunts with
a vengeance. In her mind she jumped over any
and all inconvenient facts with the effortless-
ness of a cat jumping over a fence, and nothing,
reckoned Sam Knebelkamp, attested to this fact
better than the present occasion. What, really,
were these three supposed triumphs the family were celebrating here with Norma Jeane?
Firstly, yes, she'd won a movie contract—but

one which now appeared to be fraught with moral dangers. Secondly, yes, she'd gained the companionship of a sister—but one whose husband was showing no desire to move to LA, so that Berniece and Mona Rae would soon have to go back home to Tennessee. And thirdly, yes, Norma Jeane had obtained her Nevada divorce—but in so doing she was throwing away not only a kinder and fitter husband than she was ever likely meet again but also the man she still claimed to love!

Aunt Ana, to whom everyone had looked, said nothing. But her eyes—glistening with kindness above an immense but wilting lace ruffle at the collar of her freshly ironed though well-worn dress—turned to Sam with a look that pierced his conscience slightly by the utterly selfless example it offered. She had no need of saying any words in front of Norma Jeane, having said them so many times to the others, about why this precious fatherless child had been thrust into their hands in the hour of Gladys Baker's defeat. The wise Aunt Ana, in her silence and without at all intending it, could cause Sam to scan his own ebbing past and wonder where amidst the crush of its countless hard decisions he might have failed in playing some vital part for Norma Jeane. Too, by her mere untroubled gaze, Ana could reinforce on the minds of everyone present this thing which she'd always foretold: *that in the end, all was going to be well with Norma Jeane.* More than just well—she was going to become famous. She was going to become beautiful. She was going to become a star. And not for nothing was this so, for beautiful creatures attracted attention, and attention gave one the power to work in the world for the good. Her beauty would open a pathway to the Divine. Make no mistake about it, the great Aunt Ana had averred, Norma Jeane's light was meant to shine to the ends of the earth—and in so doing it would touch, for the good and in no small way, the hearts of even the world's downtrodden and dispossessed.

Norma Jeane heard none of all this but only saw written in the faces of all three of her Atchinson aunts a starry-eyed force which nothing coming from Sam Knebelkamp could ever question or gainsay. She was going to be a star. This was no mere dream or fantasy on the women's part. It was a *fact* to which they happened to be privy—a destiny inscribed with absolute certainty on the Scroll of Life.

"Oh, I feel so good!" cooed Norma Jeane as the waiter brought in the first of the entrees to the quietly listening Berniece and Mona Rae. "Things like a little hassle with an agent are just part of the business—"

Pausing with delight upon that thought, Norma Jeane then saucily added, "—*my* business."

This last emphasis was meant for the skeptical ears of her mother Gladys—whose business indeed it had once also been—who with Aunt Grace had once not only held her own at the skilled and exacting craft of negative film cutting, but on the side had also pored over fan magazines for hours on end, and with Aunt Grace had stood entranced in the thickest of the crowds at Hollywood premieres. But all that had happened in a time before the disastrous metaphysical hurricane had passed directly over her head and left her the changed woman she was today whose job was to pin tags on clothes in a department store downtown for a pittance of her former pay.

Perfectly oblivious to her daughter's gibe, Gladys Baker only continued to wait impassively for her dinner plate.

CHAPTER SEVENTEEN

Arcing Wave

It might be just fine for a Jane Russell or a Bob Mitchum. Both those earlier close acquaintances of Jim Dougherty's had hides thick enough to fend off Hollywood's nastiest tricks and blows. But Norma Jeane had no such protection. Anyone who wanted to crush her could do so with the slightest rudeness. During their marriage Jim had needed to be constantly on the lookout for it, whether coming from himself or from others.

His deepening conviction on the subject had bothered the twenty-four-year-old sailor as he disembarked at the San Francisco harbor and had continued to bother him as he took the train southward to Los Angeles. Arriving there, he sought out Aunt Ana, whom he arranged to meet at an hour when she was alone at the Nebraska Street house. But in pouring out his fears to her, he discovered a woeful blind spot in the dear old woman's otherwise lofty thinking. "She seemed awestruck," he would later write, "by the very notion that Norma Jeane might become a movie star." No argument on Jim's part could shake the deep presentiments Aunt Ana seemed to harbor in this regard, nor cure her of a naive assumption that stardom— should anyone as unprepared as Norma Jeane ever manage to attain such a goal—spelled automatic happiness for the girl.

Similarly, when a dispirited Dougherty brought his signed divorce documents over to Norma Jeane a day or two later, he found her in extraordinarily high if, he thought, illusionary spirits. Mercifully for Jim, her state of elation had nothing to do with the papers he held out to her at her front door. She barely even glanced down at these. Instead there was news she was bursting to tell him—two things left unmentioned by Aunt Ana in order that her niece might break them to Jim herself. 20th Century-Fox, she gushed, had now made it official. In the weeks since he'd been away at sea, her contract—the one that had been pending the last time they'd spoken—had been signed by the studio! She was in training to become a movie star! Furthermore, they'd even given her a new name!

Jim's first reaction was to scornfully say in his own mind, *So what the hell does she think I care about all that?*! But clearly he did care about it, because it felt as if a bar of red-hot iron were burning a hole from his heart down to his belly. And what seemed damned remarkable to him was that Norma Jeane could stand there without the slightest inkling of what he felt—that she actually expected him to rejoice with her about this news!

"What'll they be calling you?" he asked her, adopting out of pride the most neutral and detached attitude he could muster as he placed the ignored papers down atop the little table just inside her door.

"From now on, Jimmie," she beamed, "I'll be called Marilyn Monroe."

"What?" In no way did this bizarre concoction of syllables correspond with his idea of Norma Jeane Dougherty.

She repeated, "Marilyn Monroe," and kept looking up at him expectantly.

"Where'd they dream that name up—Marilyn Monroe?"

Norma Jeane hastily proffered a story to the effect that the first name had come from one of her grandmothers and the last name from the other one. Jim could easily recall having heard about her grandmother Della Monroe before, but it was news to him that she now claimed to have a second grandmother by any name sounding so recently coined as *Marilyn*. Asked Norma Jeane, "What do you think of it?"

Jim turned the strange sounds over in his mind for a moment before hesitantly conceding, "It's—beautiful..." Which was a thing he could probably say honestly if he considered the name apart from anyone he knew. At the word "beautiful," Norma Jeane's expression changed to her broadest grin. "Isn't it the most beautiful name you ever heard?!" she cried. "It's just so, *so* beautiful!" Breaking into a dance of joy, she sang out the name, "Marilyn Monroe!—Marilyn Monroe!" Momentarily she stopped and looked back up at him. "Oh Jimmie, please, tell me you like the name! It's important to me that you like it. Please! What do you think of it?"

All Jim could wonder was, *Here she is, having dumped our marriage, having dumped* me *in effect. Why should it matter to her now what I think of her crazy new name? Yet without question it matters to her!* And dutifully he repeated aloud, "It's just beautiful."

Norma Jeane lifted her arms over her head and began twirling about the room. Her face beamed with happiness as she sang out the name over and over again in her clear, sweet voice, "Marilyn Monroe! Marilyn Monroe! Isn't it just too perfect?!" In so doing, she glided past stacks of magazines lying on various counters and tables, all of them bearing pictures of her, either on their covers or—as Jim had found out on his earlier stay in her apartment—filling their inside pages. "Marilyn Monroe! Oh, isn't it lovely?!"

Jim had seen Norma Jeane carried away by joy before, but never like this. The scene was becoming, in fact, surreal. Before him was a whirling, swaying, chanting, blonde-haired creature in whom he no longer recognized any trace of the shy, chestnut-haired, prematurely sensible sixteen-year-old Norma Jeane he'd once married. It called to mind a certain image he'd been entertaining on shipboard during the past few weeks, which today seemed to be coming true right in front of his eyes. What he'd visualized, there on the ship, was the whole arc of their relationship in the form of a giant ocean wave that had crashed ashore and engulfed the two of them in passionate love for three or four delirious years—but was now sliding back out to sea again and with it was taking her away from him forever. In real life, at this moment, his darling Norma Jeane seemed to him, for the first time now, truly and utterly gone.

Jim turned to leave. Norma Jeane's dancing stopped, and they walked out onto the porch together. She continued to beam with delight. He looked down at her and, with effort, smiled too. He wanted to reach out for her, but for a second all he could manage was the smile. Then suddenly he did reach out for her—only just as suddenly to pull back again. He thought he could feel tears wetting his cheeks. He hoped his voice would sound normal when he said goodbye. What came out was just a rough growl as he walked away.

To be sure, Norma Jeane had offered to still live with him even while divorced. And of course that offer had been very tempting to Jim Dougherty. However, his pride, his morals, his plans, and his decision of mind were such that she could only be a memory to him now—albeit a memory he still loved so much that sometimes he felt his heart would burst asunder.

CHAPTER EIGHTEEN

Mimosa Blossoms

Berniece Miracle could detect no reason for holding Jim Dougherty in anything less than the highest esteem. And for that matter, neither did Norma Jeane claim to love him any less now than she'd ever done before. Yet despite everything Berniece kept hearing about her personable ex-brother-in-law, somehow she never got to meet the young sailor when he was known to be home on leave between his troop-hauling stints from the Far East. Exactly why Norma Jeane—or *Marilyn*, as she now insisted on being called—made no real effort to bring the two of them together, considering how amicable were the terms still in place between her and Jim, only some lapse in her normally good manners could quite explain. But Berniece adjusted to this oversight without complaint. It only brought home to her how thoroughly Marilyn was distracted by the career hopes smoldering beneath her deceptively quiet exterior like so much red-hot magma about to blow the top off a long-dormant volcano.

More disquieting, however, was another lapse that came to light toward the end of Berniece's several months' stay in Los Angeles. The sisters were on a break during one of the last of their sightseeing jaunts, sipping Cokes in the chic coffee shop just off the Ambassador Hotel's posh main lobby, when Marilyn announced, "I have something on mm-my mm-mm-mind I want you to know about."

Her slight stutter had momentarily reappeared.

"What is it, honey?" Berniece asked.

"I p-posed nude for a photographer."

The silence that followed—though an exceedingly brief one—carried an effect on Berniece not unlike the distant, low, crackling rumble lately being presented over the radio as the recorded sound of one of the actual atomic bombs that had brought a miraculous and horrific end to war in the Pacific.

"Really?" Berniece said reflexively, not having any idea what she could possibly say next.

Certainly this was news outlandish in the extreme. In a rush, walls and foundations were crumbling and collapsing all across the seemly tableau that until now had been serving in Berniece's head to depict Marilyn's professional world. Starting with a certain much-talked-of shrine which the two of them had just been strolling out over the palatial hotel's lush lawns and gardens to see—the Blue Book Agency and Modeling School. There, hardly more than a year ago, in a bungalow of offices charmingly set amidst the lemon and orange and banana trees that clustered along walk-ways scented with jasmine and mimosa blos-soms, Norma Jeane's life had first undergone its daring transformation. In that time, to be sure, plenty of magazine covers had rolled off the presses bearing her growingly famil-iar image. But how quickly it had all come to this! Was it possible for Blue Book's presiding genius, Miss Emmeline Snively, to be mixed up in anything sounding so gauche?—Miss Snively, with her discreet British accent and her exquisitely white-gloved hands?!

Of course, it was all about money. Money being that troublesome commodity Marilyn was constantly running out of. No one anywhere near the girl could ignore her woeful ineptitude at the handling of her finances, which until this present moment had been Berniece's only seri-ous worry regarding her younger sister's fledg-ling career. Almost never could Marilyn give any credible accounting for where her money was going. Admittedly her seventy-five dollars a week from Fox was no star's salary, but working girls her age all over America were living perfectly well on far less. And here was Marilyn, perpetually broke and always having to take these modeling jobs on the side to make ends meet. Probably now she'd gotten herself into some frightful new jam over another debt and had figured that her only way out of it was by compromising everything.

Oh honey! thought Berniece.

Marilyn's large blue-gray eyes—the beautifully wide-set eyes that were perhaps what really made hers the face of a model and starlet—were leveled coolly on Berniece. It was as if she could see the thoughts running through her companion's mind and had no respect for them.

"I'm not ashamed," Marilyn stated with confidence, her stutter now completely gone. "I did it, and that's that. But I don't want Aunt Ana to know. She wouldn't approve."

Berniece quickly checked her dismay and managed to rejoin, "Well, maybe Aunt Ana won't see the pictures. Why should she? Would someone show them to her? I really doubt that possibility. What—what magazine will they be in?"

"I don't know. I guess the photographer will let me know," answered Marilyn. Then, exhaling a conclusive breath, she composed her face into an attractive smile. This was a signal that they wouldn't be delving any further into the subject right now. And if Marilyn was like their mother Gladys in any one thing, it was that you couldn't invade certain sectors of her mind when she'd decided to hold them private and apart. Everyone—all the aunts and uncles and even Gladys herself—knew and respected this. "You're right," continued Marilyn. "I shouldn't worry. Ana may never see the pictures. I'll decide what to do about it if it ever happens."

During that moment's revelation, each of the sisters had taken a giant step toward the other in a spirit of sisterhood. But suddenly each had seen an abyss yawning between them. And each had cautiously stepped backward again.

CHAPTER NINETEEN

Voice from Olympus

"Please, could I keep my mother's maiden name?!" blurted out Norma Jeane on stepping into Ben Lyon's office one afternoon in late November. He'd asked her to come by. She would be making a public appearance for the studio tonight, so the last possible minute had come to write an end to their charade over her screen name.

Lyon deliberated Norma Jeane's plea—or appeared to do so, for he'd known all along that he was going to give her what she wanted. And

Monroe was the perfect last name anyway. That had been abundantly clear to him for months, ever since the day Hugh Harrison, upstairs in Publicity, had dreamed up the melodious first name of *Marilyn* to go along with it. The first and last names went together like a pair of silken gloves, and together they set the starlet off as becomingly as had the solid-sequined gown she'd worn for her screen test. The surname *Monroe*—were Lyon to now try and rationalize what one can really only divine by happy instinct—added just the sober and dignified note needed to counterweight the childlikeness of her face and expression. Ironically the elevation and propriety of *Monroe* was also needed to offset a certain sheer physicality always playing dangerously close to the surface in the way she moved her body. This latter characteristic in fact had been pronounced too downright raw by no less an authority than Darryl F. Zanuck, whom Lyon could foresee having to coax at option time merely to keep Norma Jeane under contract. The capricious studio boss, initially impressed by her silent screen test, had turned skeptical upon sizing her up in person. Everything about her manner and even about her voice had struck the all-powerful head of production as too unsophisticated for the Fox roster.

Marilyn Monroe. Maybe the name would help, reasoned Ben Lyon, who on the contrary and quite aside from any personal grounds he might have for being excited about the girl, considered her to be no run-of-the-mill stock player. Whatever her qualities off-camera, the screen test had shown her capable of an on-camera allure that might even take her as far as stardom—depending of course on a host of other things—on her improvement under coaching, on the story properties coming their way for production, on how he might contrive to get her cast in them, on whether or not producers liked her, even on the future career whims of Betty Grable, whose replacement Norma

Jeane might in time conceivably become. And not least under the mysterious laws of the game, casting Norma Jeane in the role of a star depended on selecting the right name. But this, curiously, the girl had already managed to do for herself.

Not that Ben Lyon needed to tell her so right away. He rather enjoyed the way she leaned toward him from a chair opposite his desk, a look of desperate entreaty filling her wide blue eyes. He wondered, *What a thing of urgency this is to her! It makes the situation appear almost comedic. Has she no appreciation for how many other girls— girls far prettier, far more poised and more prepared than she, although possibly less talented than she in her one special way—come and go within the great walls of 20th Century-Fox in the course of a single month or year?* Nevertheless, Ben Lyon carefully suppressed any show of mirth. It appealed to the actor in him to play all his interviews with pretty young screen hopefuls for the big scenes the girls themselves imagined them to be. With immense gravity, therefore, he now sat back in his chair, leaned his chin on one hand, and studied every part of Norma Jeane's anatomy while secretly savoring the profound excitement this scrutiny aroused in her. It was obvious she'd poured not just hours but days and weeks into planning for, into daydreaming of, this one crucial exchange between them. For several long moments he said nothing, and her quickened breathing was the only sound in the room. Then suddenly, with an air of momentous decision, he spoke out in his large voice still well-known to millions of movie and radio fans, as if he were thundering down a wondrous new appellation from the heights of Mount Olympus. "All right, *Monroe's* in," he announced. "It was good enough for a president. We'll use it."

A tiny murmur of inarticulate relief escaped from Norma Jeane.

But Lyon, lest she say some word to break his concentration, quickly raised the forfending palm of his hand and knitted his brow with magisterial concern to pursue in a zinging voice, "Now for a first name."

The valiant Norma Jeane stirred not a muscle, but Lyon saw the blood draining out of her face. She'd calculated the rest of the battle as already won, he perceived, given that she'd been beguiling him privately into calling her *Marilyn* for months. Thus secure in having reduced the starlet to utter defeat, Lyon now mercifully deigned to raise her up again by spinning impulsively round in his chair, springing to his feet, and pacing back and forth behind his desk in order to probe the farthest reaches of his fertile memory in search of the two choicest and most dazzling among all the possible options for a first name. There were, he finally told the increasingly suspense-wracked starlet, two women of whom she reminded him. He'd known them both extremely well. One was the luminous Jean Harlow, his costar in Howard Hughes' illustrious and landmark 1930 talkie

Hell's Angels. The other was Broadway's dazzling singer, dancer, and comedienne Marilyn Miller, whom he'd romanced on screen in her starring vehicle of 1931, *Her Majesty, Love.*

Jean? Or *Marilyn*? Which name did she prefer? The choice was hers.

Norma Jeane cast her eyes downward while pressing a forefinger against her lips, hesitating in the way she frequently did before voicing any important thought. Lyon's gaze fell on her long, glistening golden hair so like Marilyn Miller's. Truth be told, from the first moment that the name *Marilyn* had been broached for Norma Jeane, she'd become in his eyes a virtual reincarnation of Marilyn Miller, whom Lyon had passionately loved before marrying his present wife. Perhaps the twenty-year-old Norma Jeane had divined something of this. Or perhaps it was simply that he'd endearingly called her *Marilyn* one too many times, so that she no longer had any doubts about which name he himself liked best. At any rate,

thought Lyon, here was why Darryl F. Zanuck
might be wrong in his assessment of Norma
Jeane Dougherty. At this moment—even if it
would have killed her not to come into pos-
session of the name *Marilyn*—she hesitated
because there was a chance of upping her ante.
She saw this chance and threw the dice. Yes,
Lyon had found Norma Jeane to be an awkward and peculiar girl in many ways, a loner, a
dreamer, difficult to read, difficult to connect
with, someone having a long hard road ahead
of her to travel. But there was a mettle to this
girl that he'd never seen in any aspirant her
age before. Instead of desperately seizing on
the clear opportunity being dangled in front
of her, in her shrewdness she recognized that it
never looked good for an ingénue to do all the
plumping for herself. She wanted the record
to show it was the studio that had named her
Marilyn Monroe.

Norma Jeane glanced trustfully at Lyon,
who said to himself: *OK, this is the way it works*

in Hollywood. Norma Jeane has done plenty for me. Now it's my turn to do for her.

"You are to me a Marilyn," he prompted her in his low and mellifluous voice.

The reassurance contained in these words emboldened the starlet to pull out all the rest of the stops in her embellishment of the scene to be played.

It was a lovely name, she agreed. Yet she wasn't totally convinced. It still had a strange ring to it. Would *Marilyn* perhaps sound too artificial? Maybe she'd better just take the name *Jean,* which, after all, was one of her own given names?

"*Marilyn* goes better with *Monroe* than *Jean,*" countermanded Lyon without hesitation. "It's got a nicer flow—with the two M's. *Marilyn Monroe*. Say it."

"Mm-mm—" Norma Jeane began, suddenly evincing the slight stutter that now and then came upon her rather appealingly out of nowhere.

They both began to laugh. She tried again.

"That's it!" Lyon clapped his hands when she succeeded in pronouncing the name. "What do you think, sweetheart?"

"Well," sighed the starlet, "I guess I'm Marilyn Monroe."

CHAPTER TWENTY

Parade of the Stars

Under the magic of night several hours later, the studio's float pulled onto a Hollywood Boulevard illuminated like fairyland for the opening of the Christmas shopping season.

"This is the end of Norma Jeane," would write Marilyn years afterward of this epochal moment in her life. For there was only one all-important community left in which she'd had no choice but to allow the old name still to cling to her, and that had been at the studio. But tonight it was the powers that be of no less prestigious an entity than 20th Century-Fox Pictures itself who were sending word out to the entire world in the form of a glittering sign which somebody in the art department had hastily hand-painted and jauntily affixed next to the seat now holding the starlet aloft in one of America's most dazzling parades. Tonight it was official. She was Marilyn Monroe.

Spectators by the thousands upon thousands lined the route of Hollywood's Parade of the Stars. Her stomach pounded. Her head felt dizzy. Her voice completely left her. Such was the reaction she'd always experienced when faced with an audience—*any* audience, even if only that of her own little family poised around a large restaurant table, directing smiles at her that were meant to be encouraging but which seemed edged with an uneasy formality and expectation. Whereas here was an audience stretching visibly for more than a mile in front of her, a veritable sea of faces on both sides of the boulevard, punctuated by myriads of glistening eyes that turned toward her in waves out of the shadows as Fox's float proceeded from one shining Hollywood landmark to the next. And yet the first of the grand movie palaces which they passed, the magnificent Pantages, had barely disappeared behind them as the gigantic old Warner Brothers Theater rolled into view two blocks further down, when she perceived that these countless eyes belonged not to strangers at all but to a warm presence already quite familiar to her from her daydreams. Far from threatening, they comforted her. They were a million anonymous human cameras clicking away contentedly in the semidarkness. And Marilyn, having recently put in two years as a photographer's model, could say unequivocally there was no place in the world she'd rather be than in front of cameras.

So lulled, somewhere in the twenty-year-old starlet's mind, a door opened through which she easily glided to find herself alone with the secret child of her past.

Who in all this audience guessed how she'd come to this moment only through a terrible year spent just one short block away from this spot—in a school building unseen behind the stores now passing her on the left-hand side? Not that her little second-grade classroom at the Selma Street School had been in itself so terrible, since it had given her some of the few kindly hours of human anchoring she'd managed to know that entire year. Nor could she ever forget that it was during that same year's sojourn in Hollywood that certain facts had been made known to her—that certain revelations had been passed down to her as it were, one through her mother Gladys and the other through her Aunt Grace—which she still treasured as heirlooms beyond any price. No, it was the saving peculiarity of the memories slipping so readily into place in her mind tonight that it had taken her twelve years of hindsight to assemble them in their true and terrible light.

Luckily shielding the seven-year-old Norma Jeane from the brunt of such reflections had been the fabulous refuge coming up next along that same left-hand side of the boulevard. From her perch aboard the Fox float, Marilyn could glimpse the Egyptian Theater's colorfully muraled walls at the far end of its long, jungle-like forecourt. How many Saturday afternoons had she spent under the splendid sunburst ceiling inside, sitting all alone at the exact center of the very front row? So totally would every image up on the screen seize her attention that she'd sit here through the same movie two and three times over. Until finally, stabbed by a reawakening consciousness of a parallel reality awaiting her elsewhere, she'd be forced to emerge from that wonderful temple of the imagination, sometimes only after dark.

And just here too along Hollywood Boulevard, but on the opposite side of Fox's float in the second story over the sidewalk, rose the palazzo windows of a place she'd only heard talked about at the age of seven, but which today she recognized as virtually the soil out of which Norma Jeane had sprung—the once-jumping Montmartre Café. It had been, during her mother Gladys' and her Aunt Grace's heyday, the *in* spot for wild nights on the town. Here, more than once no doubt, the two flirtatious film cutters had dined and danced and sought to rub elbows with the stars. How improbable was it then for Marilyn to speculate as to whether her own first alighting onto the human scene might not have been signaled here by a proverbial twinkle in Stanley Gifford's eye?

For that was the name of the gentleman who still haunted her in a thousand daydreams. She'd known him principally by means of an enormously appealing photograph which that year Gladys had kept enshrined on Norma Jeane's bedroom wall. To reach the hallowed spot where it had hung, her frequent way home from school had lain via a path that diverged from tonight's parade route at the large and busy intersection coming up next just ahead. Tonight Marilyn's view in the direction little Norma Jeane had taken home was going to be obscured by choking crowds, by wintertime's darkness overhead, and by an unprecedented glare of holiday lights from the Boulevard. But amidst the everyday bustle at Highland Avenue's crossing, the child would turn right and trudge uphill a short curving distance to tiny Arbol Street at the foot of Cahuenga Pass. The house they'd once owned there was still standing—Marilyn had just been back to see it in the past month or two with Berniece and Aunt Grace—a pretty white place with a Greek portico front and a white picket fence surrounding the yard.

Photographically, C. Stanley Gifford's warm presence suffusing that all-important house on Arbol Street had been rather like what emanated now from the sea of faces turning to regard Marilyn as her float entered the packed intersection of Hollywood and Highland. Moreover,

like each of the persons making up tonight's
crowds, Gifford had been without any name to
Norma Jeane at that early stage of her aware-
ness. Nonetheless, his bright mysterious eyes,
ironical yet hugely reassuring under the tipped
brim of his fedora, had seemed to keep contin-
ual watch over her from his framed picture high
on the wall. She'd always clearly understood
that he was her father. That unspeakably precious fact had been among the few such treas-
ures Gladys Baker had ever managed to confide
to Norma Jeane.

Immediately now on the starlet's right-
hand side, three more places whirled past in
quick succession to tantalize her with her last
remembered glimpses of the mother who'd
shared with her that confidence, of the mother
who later might have shared with her incal-
culably more had everything not changed and
had Gladys not become instead a light extin-
guished, a sparkling presence permanently
crushed out. This world-changing loss had all

been accomplished within a single year, right here before her eyes as a small child. Yet such was the durability of hope that only in the past couple of months had she finally accepted that loss as a fully grown woman. With the result that tonight she passed these places making only one fervent prayer—that just because Hollywood and Highland had been the cross-roads of Norma Jeane's world for one year did not mean it had to be the crossroads of Marilyn Monroe's mind forever—that by putting on her new name she was now putting off all the scars of that past.

She could clearly recall their strolling round this corner during the lightsome summer of 1933, past the fancy entrance driveway to the first and mightiest of the three addresses, the massive old Hollywood Hotel. Gladys had still been talkative then—vibrantly and cleverly so, especially when animated by the presence of Aunt Grace, who most often came along on their Sunday evening walks to C.C. Brown's for ice cream. On such evenings the two women had chattered much of the fabled hotel whose mission-style gables and churrigueresque bell towers had overlooked the surrounding lemon groves and barley fields as long ago as the very year when Gladys' own parents, the ill-starred Otis and Della Monroe, had first brought Gladys as a mere infant to southern California. However, it was the hostelry's later and more citified decades that had most fascinated Gladys and Grace. Their heads were filled with stories about the many idols of the silent screen who'd wined and partied and honeymooned in the hotel well into the days and nights of the two women's own vivid recollection as workers and players themselves on the frenzied Hollywood scene.

Then, of course, right next door to the Hollywood Hotel was to rise the most famous theater in the world, the towering Grauman's Chinese, which happened to have been a-building just while Gladys Baker had been pregnant with Norma Jeane and still preoccupied with the grief of Stanley Gifford's choosing not to marry her. But by the time Norma Jeane herself came to know these places—seven years after that in 1933—the recovered Gladys had been able to laugh quite merrily as their little company of three had enjoyed sundaes and floats at the storied ice cream parlor located yet one further door down Hollywood Boulevard. Indeed good fortune, for the moment, had seemed to be smiling on them. Both Gladys and Grace, despite the horrendously hard times sweeping across America, were holding good jobs in a glamorous industry town that so far appeared to have outwitted the Great Depression. Gladys, in fact, was successfully juggling jobs at two studios in order keep up payments on her steeply mortgaged new home. The observant little Norma Jeane, it was true, hadn't failed to notice that even on their most buoyant Sunday outings, her mother never embraced her nor even smiled at her in the solicitous, heartwarming way the girl had often seen other mothers do with their children. But sometimes, sitting in the pleasant wooden booths of C.C. Brown's, Norma Jeane had been allowed to rest her head against the shoulder of the still young, delicately beautiful, red-haired Gladys while dreaming to the lilting cadence of the ladies' rapid voices. And this at the time had felt like enough.

It must have been just weeks after those memories, around the start of Norma Jeane's school year that fall, that the terrible thing had first begun coming over her mother. In truth, lined up and awaiting turns to strike the poor woman out of a clear blue sky had been a row of thunderbolts, an array of misfortunes so exquisitely timed as if meant purposely to destroy her, this unholy assault lasting four or five months during which time not even Aunt Grace had fully comprehended what manner of war her friend was waging. Norma Jeane of course had understood far less, seeing only its very end result.

That result, those four or five months later, had come shortly after Christmas. The child had been sitting in the kitchen at her breakfast with an English couple who'd been sharing the house on Arbol Street, when Gladys had suddenly begun shrieking from the living room couch that someone was coming down the stairs to kill her. The couple had restrained Norma Jeane from running out to her mother. What had come next was the most frightful noise the child had ever heard—unforgettable crashing and thuds that, together with Gladys' screaming and laughter, had kept up so long and so violently that the Englishman had finally called for the police. A short while later, an ambulance had come to take Gladys away.

Little noted at the time—little noted, that is, by anyone out loud—was that Gladys' fears of bodily harm hadn't been totally unfounded. Union strikes plaguing movieland during several previous months had engulfed her film-cutting jobs for a long enough time to threaten

Gladys literally with the loss of her home. The hapless young mother, facing in this the collapse of a life's plan which she deemed almost akin to sacred, had recently been caught by a photographer in the act of climbing over a fence to evade the picket lines and get back to her work at RKO. The result had been her picture in the newspaper's city pages, and her identity potentially made as clear as day to union goons not known for dealing tenderly with strike-breaking members.

But during those same intervening months and equally unbeknownst to Norma Jeane, other thunderbolts too had helped unhinge her mother's mind. One of them traced to a grandfather back in Missouri, namely Della Monroe's kind and sensitive father Tilford Hogan, who in the spring of that worst and deepest year of the Great Depression had succumbed to despair at the loss of his health and of his farm and had thrown a rope over a high rafter in the barn and hung himself. This was a shock Gladys might well have worked her way through in safety if only the news of it hadn't been delayed in reaching her until the fall—for by then other news had reached her too which had struck a thousand times closer to her heart. Her dear and firstborn child, her only son Jackie, who had been stolen from her ten years before along with little Berniece and carried off by their father to Kentucky—that boy who'd secretly stood centermost in her dreams for the house on Arbol Street—was suddenly revealed to be lost to Gladys forever, having perished half a continent away in extreme agony from a kidney infection at the age of fifteen.

For as long a time as it was a question of her son Jackie's death and Jackie's alone, Gladys Baker had handled her situation with remarkable self-containment. Many weeks had passed after her getting word the boy was gone during which she'd allowed nothing in her outward life to change. With *Flying Down to Rio* in front of the cameras at RKO and *It Happened One Night* just swinging into production at Columbia in the fall of 1933, she'd continued to hold down her positions at both studios, throwing herself upon the sympathies of no one and keeping always to the same aloof distance from acquaintances and co-workers that they'd long taken to be a sovereign mark of her subtly attractive persona. In view of her recent loss, they could only judge her to be a tower of strength.

Among these admiring colleagues, Aunt Grace had been alone in realizing that her dearest friend was in fact groping desperately within herself for some stratagem not to sink into a pit of frank despair. This was knowledge that the intensely private Gladys wouldn't and couldn't have imparted by word of mouth to any living soul, but it was there plainly to be discerned by the woman who for more than ten years had stood as an avid diplomat between Gladys' cryptic reserve and the flashier abandon of most of their compeers—by the woman who might even have been called Gladys Baker's creator. For

it was Grace McKee who'd in large part engi-
neered the smarter styles, the bolder coloration,
and the foxier bearing that had transformed a
slightly haughty note about Gladys' manner
into a full-blown mystique credible in the eyes
of Hollywood's beau monde. Thus it was now
Aunt Grace alone who'd known how to read a
subtle change in the language of Gladys' slen-
der torso as she sat poised at her cutting-room
table. Who'd known how to gauge a certain
slackening in the deftness with which Gladys'
cotton-gloved hands regulated the reels of film
unwinding from her left-hand side and rewind-
ing to her right. Who'd observed an altered cast
about Gladys' finely made features in the glow
of the table's well-light as she quietly calculated
her frames of precious negative. Hence too,
when that device of survival desperately sought
after by Gladys had at last fallen into her ago-
nized grasp, it was for Aunt Grace alone, finding out what that device was, to recoil in horror
like a doting connoisseur upon discovering that

some priceless and much-beloved work of art had been hideously and atrociously disfigured.

The truth of it had come to light quite casually, amidst bits and strands of other, more trivial conversation. Perhaps it was all a consequence of Gladys' having clung too fixedly to her much-imperiled dream for the house on Arbol Street. Which indeed was all she'd now continued to do—however, not with just her two daughters in mind but also, still, her son! Somewhere in time, Gladys had slipped noiselessly into a state of abject denial of the cruel truth clattering at her door. She seemed honestly to believe that Jackie Baker was still alive. Hardly had it mattered if Aunt Grace might conjecture that all this was nothing more than a grandiose stunt being perpetrated by Gladys upon herself. The result, within the woman's own distracted mind, was exactly the same. A powerful vacuum had been created there— and just in time, as it now happened, to suck in the onrushing news of Tilford Hogan's act of self-destruction. Incomprehensibly it was only her grandfather's death—albeit one so belatedly learned about and one so much less relevant than Jackie's death to her immediate world—that could crack the stubborn shell of Gladys' self-deception. Accordingly, now all her faculties, heretofore forcibly idled, were set free to feed on that suicide's every unwhole-some detail. Until an idea began pressing itself on her that Tilford Hogan's last troubles sig-naled some hereditary affliction and that she too might now be losing her mind.

At length this idea had hardened into con-viction, conviction had begotten alarm, and alarm had degenerated into panic. Aunt Grace had at last sprung into action. Thinking only to head off disaster by the means most in vogue with her industry's smart set, she'd called in a Santa Monica neurologist. But, alas, that doc-tor's fashionable nostrums had proven just another in the line of thunderbolts waiting to strike Gladys out of a clear blue sky. Her fragile system had rejected his pharmacological intrusion with the wildest violence.

The ambulance clearly remembered by Norma Jeane had carried the ravaged woman off to a rest home in Santa Monica. From there she would soon be taken to Los Angeles General Hospital, and from there before long to Norwalk State Hospital—unluckily the very place where Gladys' mother Della happened to have died insane. And for a total of twelve years at these and succeeding institutions, doctors would strive to make Gladys Monroe Baker whole using ever more powerful treatments whose ever more powerful effects the caregivers themselves seldom appeared to understand.

Meanwhile, of course, the pretty white house on Arbol Street had been lost. Norma Jeane, in the process of its being sold, had been allowed to stay there under the care of the English couple and to finish out her second-grade year at the Selma Street school. Almost every day, Aunt Grace had come to the house on Arbol

Street to see her. Their Sunday night walks to
C.C. Brown's had continued, and Gladys Baker
had even followed along with them on certain
weekends while on temporary release from the
hospital as a check for any improvement in
her hold on reality. The three of them, just as
always after ice cream at C.C. Browns, would
stop at Grauman's Chinese Theater to pay their
respects in the forecourt where the testimoni-
als of the stars lay inscribed immemorially in
cement. Only by now, Aunt Grace had begun
transmitting to Norma Jeane the second of that
year's two great revelations—the first of them
having been Gladys' disclosure that the man of
the enshrined photograph was the girl's own
father. Aunt Grace's only thought at first, in
making her own revelation, had been somehow
to fill in for the lost mother who was after all
her own longtime dearest friend, quite apart
from any reckoning of what Grace might owe
both mother and daughter for her heavy if
unwitting role in Gladys' medical fiasco. Yet in

amazingly short order and quite mysteriously surpassing herself, Grace had already come firmly to believe every word she was saying: "Don't worry, Norma Jeane," she would whisper to the tow-headed child crouching to fit her palm over a freshly minted handprint of the dazzling Jean Harlow while the mother stood several steps behind them, looking on with an expression like a ghost. "You're going to be a *great* movie star!" thrilled Aunt Grace. "Oh, I can feel it in my bones!"

Norma Jeane had to some extent understood what this meant. Sometimes at these moments—Marilyn could remember—a vague dismay would ripple through her little frame at a prospect opening before her of something too boundless and grave and lonely to be endured. But over the span of twelve years since those evening strolls, how completely her feelings about it had changed!

A band stopped playing somewhere in front of the Fox float—or perhaps behind it. From the separated place in Marilyn's mind, she was jolted back to the present. It was November the 22nd of 1946. A raw crunching of marching feet sounded on the chilly asphalt, and far up ahead of them a thunderous cheering and applause kept going up where Roy Rogers, the King of the Cowboys, was leading off the Parade of the Stars to the clip-clopping of his horse Trigger's hooves. Meanwhile, Grauman's Chinese Theater, C. C. Brown's Ice Cream Parlor, and the Hollywood Hotel were receding into the distance behind them. *Never, never, never a word!* Marilyn vowed, looking back on the two diminutive figures of Gladys and Aunt Grace, paralyzed in her memory over the cement of the Grauman's forecourt. *Never—if Gladys had failed miserably in life and been proven hopelessly unmotherlike in everything having to do with Norma Jeane—would Marilyn utter a word against her, if only because she'd strived so valiantly, once, to make everything happen otherwise.*

But thank God for Aunt Grace!

By no means had this past faded from Marilyn's mind when the Parade of the Stars came to an end on the same Hollywood side street where it had begun. There, radio favorites Fibber McGee and Molly were scrambling down from the sleigh on which they'd soared with Santa Claus over mock-European rooftops high atop a float that had passed continually through its own self-generated snowstorm. Elsewhere up and down the little avenue, other stars were dismounting from the backs of brilliantly polished convertibles and gathering to saunter round the corner for a soiree to be held at the Brown Derby on Vine Street. Mingling with them en route to the legendary eatery were the starlets of 20th Century-Fox—for in truth, Marilyn was only one of several pretty stock players whom Ben Lyon had picked at the last minute to sit on the studio's float and wave to the crowds. The girls automatically struck up charming little exchanges with the stars among whom they passed. And speaking back to them might be a Red Skelton now all finished up with twisting his face from one madcap contortion to the next. Or a Frank Morgan no longer affecting the voice of the Wizard of Oz. Or a Judy Canova with no reason to bare her flaring buck teeth as the Ozark Nightingale. Or a Jack Benny who'd effortlessly cast off all semblance of his miserly practitioner of the farcical slow burn. Seeing these masters up close after everything she'd just remembered might easily have had the effect of dampening Marilyn's mood for the rest of the night. It was a certain aplomb they exuded *from underneath* that she most feared she'd never be able to emulate when her time came. Whether plying their craft or not—so her self-doubts ran at such moments—there was always somebody there whom they felt happy to be. Whereas who was *she* when you took away the wizardry of her makeup but an utterly unexceptional, plain-vanilla type of a girl with nothing whatever to distinguish her even from these other stock players except possibly her larger-than-average hat size!

So she might have felt this morning. But not tonight. Tonight she had a talisman to hold up against the dark comparisons assailing her from within. Tonight there was a rescue to lift and animate her mind, a reason for throwing herself with more force than ever against the bold trajectory of her future. "I had a new name, Marilyn Monroe," she would later write of this fresh idea which thrilled and captivated her by the very hugeness of its scope. "Now I had to *get born*! And this time better than before."

Minutes later, fans were rushing forward from the Brown Derby's canopied entrance and flocking round the approaching stars for their autographs. Of course Marilyn was well aware she was far from being a star. Yet often she'd found that the mere circumstance of being in full makeup—provided both its application and her feelings of the moment happened to be just right—evinced from her a capricious flair for attracting attention in public from the members of both sexes. Hence she was not altogether surprised when several adolescent boys now zeroed eagerly in on her with articles of paper to be signed. And hardly seconds had elapsed before there began to be enacted, once again, a scene straight out of her daydreams.

It was to be expected that the boys, in the act of crowding close to her with their eyes intently gathering in all the qualities of her face and body, immediately turned for her into an audience just like any other audience. She felt a thumping at her stomach. A lightness came to her head that was like a flash of light. And somewhere in her mind, a door opened onto a brightly lit place where she stood with this newly found little audience—but as far removed from the common sidewalk as if a split second had translated them all far up into one of the high, luminous corridors of the Hollywood Hotel. She stepped forward, as if toward that light. The door closed behind her once more, and altogether disappeared behind that door was the girl who since late last summer had been practicing on a notepad a signature which featured two great swirling initial M's—who when alone had been pronouncing the words *Marilyn Monroe* again and again and tasting them on her tongue like some exquisite new kind of candy—who'd allowed neither family member, friend, nor acquaintance, except at the studio, to call her by any other name.

Lost for the moment was that earlier girl in sublime forgetfulness.

While on this side of the door, as if newly created in the great brightness generated by the intense gaze of the boys and other bystanders, shone the starlet upon whom just a few hours earlier Ben Lyon had conferred a brand-new name. From somewhere, there materialized a writing pen. She held it poised for a second over the piece of paper handed to her by the first of the boys. And suddenly, on blind impulse, she turned to one of the bystanders while straining mightily to find her voice.

"How—how do you spell M-M-Marilyn?"

The astonished bystanders looked at one another as if to ask, *What circumstance could possibly explain why this lovely young thing doesn't know how to spell her own name?!*

CHAPTER TWENTY-ONE

Artichoke Queen

_____

Something big was astir at Enid Knebelkamp's. Of this her neighbor Catherine Larson felt sure as she crossed the street to Enid's for coffee one afternoon in February of 1948. A certain note in Enid's voice over the telephone had made her think it involved one or both of their respective kin—in Catherine's case her son, in Enid's case her niece—each of whom had spent a dismal 1947 struggling to make it in the movies.

"As I came up Enid's front walk," Catherine would later recall, "I noticed a pretty young blonde in shorts walking barefoot around the side of the house, looking at the plants and flowers. We didn't happen to speak just then, but as Enid and I sat chatting in the kitchen a few minutes later, this girl came in the back door, and Enid introduced her to me as her niece Marilyn."

That name, mentioned by her friend Enid in so many glamorous contexts on past afternoons, now gave Catherine a start when attached to the girl who sat down with them at the kitchen table. The Marilyn she'd been picturing was a photographer's model and aspiring actress radiant with a sleek and cosmopolitan beauty.

Oh dear, gasped Catherine to herself, *she looks like some kid fresh off the farm!*

Marilyn immediately cast her large, sensitive eyes downward, giving Catherine a disconcerting feeling that the twenty-one-year-old blonde had read her mind. Reflexively by way of restoring the situation, Catherine leaned forward and began warmly plying the girl with questions about her challenging choice of a career. But Marilyn only compounded and magnified the strong soupçon of the dairymaid about herself by turning out to be terribly shy as well. It took all of Catherine's considerable skills at small talk, along with Enid's tactful insertion of a right word here and there into her niece's frequent pauses, before conversation at the table began at last to buzz along again at anything like its former momentum.

Meanwhile, Catherine took up the task of silently calculating Marilyn's chances for stardom—for she was beginning to suspect that her own special perspective on that matter was the reason for Enid's calling her over this afternoon. Catherine had, after all, spent ten years on movie sets all around town in the capacity of her son Bobby's guardian as a juvenile actor. That experience had taught her a thing or two about what it takes to be a star. In her day she'd

chatted for hours on end with a chain-smok-
ing Vivien Leigh between setups for *Gone with
the Wind*, for one example. For another, she'd
thought nothing of having lunch with the
multitalented Ida Lupino—who in Catherine's
opinion was easily Hollywood's greatest beauty
in person, despite the unfortunate fact that her
flawlessly delicate complexion and exquisite
eyes somehow came across as "hard" on film.
It was comparisons on this high level that kept
flying through Catherine's mind in spite of herself today while the three women talked, as if to
mock what she knew to be Enid Knebelkamp's
unbounded confidence in her niece's future.

Now to be fair—Catherine had to consider—the girl sitting across from her was
barefoot and in shorts and wearing little if any
makeup. Too, objectivity required Catherine
to put out of her mind the niggling recollection that Marilyn had done most of her growing up in the famously rural confines of the San
Fernando Valley. Catherine must also beware

of overreacting to the recent absurd news of Marilyn's having been crowned California Artichoke Queen by the city fathers of the remote agricultural hub called Salinas. But despite all Catherine's striving to discount these strong impressions, she couldn't shake off her initial snap judgment: "Marilyn simply looked to me," as she would clearly remember a decade later, "for all the world like some awkward kid just in from the country who was taking in the bright lights of the big city for the first time and dreaming about getting into pictures!"

"Now mind you," Catherine would hasten to add, "she *was* a pretty girl. And also, I was to find, a very sweet one. Terribly, innocently sweet. Yes indeed, I did come to like her. But beautiful, no. Hers was only that just-scrubbed, wholesome kind of prettiness which had about it something too *commonplace*, too *raw* for Hollywood. Her whole manner of speaking and of moving was altogether undistinguished. In addition to which she came off to me as absolutely naive, entirely lacking in what you'd call preparation. Her very asking me the question 'How can I become a star?' showed me she possessed not a fraction of the sophistication needed to make a success in pictures—certainly to become a star. True, she'd already played a couple of very small parts on the screen when I met her—minor things at Fox that nobody in Hollywood had even noticed before the studio had dropped her again after only a year. And keep in mind that at this time she was doing lots of modeling, so of course I realized she had *something* to offer. But as a movie star? Oh dear me, no!"

All in good time, while Catherine made these considerations, the talk at Enid's kitchen table worked its way onto the fascinating subject of Rita Hayworth—to the troubles the sultry, red-haired queen of the Columbia lot had been giving that studio's boss Harry Cohn…how she was now planning, despite her contract with him, to embark on a grand tour of Europe as soon as

filming on *The Loves of Carmen* was completed...
how things had even gotten so bad that word was
going around town that Harry Cohen wanted to
groom some other girl to take her place...and
that Marilyn's agent had sent her Fox screen test
over to Columbia's Max Arnow...

OK, there it was. Now Catherine understood why Enid had called her over on this particular afternoon. For it happened that over the
course of her son Bobby's work for Columbia
Pictures, she—Catherine—had become quite
friendly with Max Arnow, Columbia's Director
of Casting. No doubt Enid was hoping her
friend would offer to put in good word with him
for Marilyn. Quickly and painfully, Catherine
thought through this question and came to her
decision: *Well, maybe I could try to say something
nice about Marilyn without compromising myself.
Obviously, keeping credibility with Max is my first
responsibility for as long as Bobby keeps having such
a tough time of it making his transition into adult
roles...*

Not two weeks later—to Catherine Larson's utter amazement—Marilyn was signed for a starring role in Columbia's *Ladies of the Chorus*. Of course it was only a B picture in black and white, a cheapie destined for nothing more conspicuous than the lower half of a double bill in a decidedly secondary tier of hinterland movie theaters. And in actual fact, the little picture ended up playing almost nowhere upon its release the following October, by which time Marilyn had already been dropped by Columbia after only six months on the payroll. So Catherine Larson, whose confidence in herself had been momentarily shaken, came to feel fully vindicated once again in her earlier judgment of Marilyn's prospects on the screen.

"We'd meet occasionally for coffee at Enid's over the next two or three years," she was later to recall. "During all that time, Marilyn's heart kept right on burning with the same question, 'How can I become a star?' Well, as I say, she was a very sweet girl. But such a naive thing—looking at me with those big innocent eyes exactly the way a very small child would. It was very strange, but you almost wanted to put her on your knee and cuddle her just as you would do with a little daughter of your own. You wanted to protect her. You wanted to tell her *life was OK*, that everything was going to be all right. Most of all, what I really felt like doing was taking her aside somewhere—on account of Enid's being there, who had such abundant faith in Marilyn's future on the screen—and saying to her, 'Look, kid, why don't you try something else? It's just not going to be worth it. You'll never make it in Hollywood.' Yes, I felt so very strongly I ought to tell her that. But of course I never did it because of Enid."

CHAPTER TWENTY-TWO

Blonde of the Day

"I was strolling down Gower Avenue in Hollywood one August afternoon in 1951"— so might a peerless observer of the passing Hollywood scene, Charles Williams, be coaxed to reveal to some carefully chosen listener many years afterward—"when a glamorously dressed blonde drove up in a convertible and parked at the opposite curb. She got out in a big hurry and crossed diagonally toward me, heading for the back entrance to RKO Studios.

"Now, see how your mind does things to you?" Charles would ask with the scene materializing before his eyes as though it had just happened yesterday. "Looking more closely at this bosomy, wide-hipped girl, I was very unimpressed. Her makeup was too heavy. She had a rather puggish nose. The outer corners of her large eyes slanted downward toward her cheekbones with an effect I didn't care for. I noticed a tacky wrinkle across the front of her skirt below a prominent tummy. She was pigeon-toed in one foot. And she was a little on the frantic side—everything about her seemed exaggerated. I said to myself, *This girl's obviously trying to be the next Lana Turner, but she's of a lesser vintage.*"

On saying this, Charles might lean in to you confidentially and add a momentary aside laughingly as if from one star-worshiper to another: "Lana was the blonde of the day, you know, and *how dare* anyone try to imitate her!

"Well," he would then say in redoubling his concentration on the scene, "she got to the RKO entrance just as I approached. And stepping up on the platform, she looked in my direction and said, very sweetly, 'Hello!'"

At this point it was again necessary for Charles to lean in toward you, but this time altogether seriously. "Now, being black," he would confide, "with Jim Crow still in full sway, I got overlooked *a lot* in those days. And here was this nice woman greeting me so politely! Of course I didn't let on what I'd been thinking but spoke back to her just as pleasantly.

"She continued to look at me," Charles would tell. "Then she pressed the buzzer—a loud one even from the outside—BOOOP!—and stood there waiting, still watching me. I'd gotten just a few feet past her when I heard the studio door open behind me. Two men's voices cried out 'Marilyn!' I whirled around. Instantly everything fell into place: 'My God,' I said to myself, 'It's Marilyn Monroe!'"

"In 1951?" Charles's listener, if an extremely astute one, might here break in to ask skeptically.

Charles would raise a finger. "Remember, stargazing was my vocation in life. I'd come out to LA from Wichita, Kansas, just to hang around the studios in hopes of seeing an Ava Gardner or an Errol Flynn. I read the *LA Times'* theatrical section every day, knew who everybody was, went to all the movies. Two years earlier I'd seen Marilyn's hottest piece of work to date, *The Asphalt Jungle*, and thought she was definitely on the rise. Then I'd seen the great *All About Eve*, plus each of those lesser-featured bits as they came out—*Love Nest*, *As Young as You Feel*, and the rest. So all this was what swept through my mind on hearing her first name."

Charles would take in an impressive breath and then continue his story.

"Well, all of a sudden, this awkward blonde who was trying to imitate Lana Turner *completely disappeared* for me. And into focus—came Marilyn Monroe! My God, she totally came alive! The reason for it being partly too that she'd recognized these two handsome, young executive types who were stepping out the door in their high-fashion suits and ties, both carrying briefcases. Fox attorneys perhaps? I didn't know who they were, but right away the two were all over her, drinking her in and trying to hold her there in conversation. She kept saying, 'But I'm late! I'm late!' and pushing at the door, trying to go in. Yet she was charmed enough by these two gentlemen to give them, for one moment, what they expected of Marilyn Monroe—throwing her head back, smiling wide, eyes half-closed, and pivoting from one foot to the other as she spoke to them in that little-girl voice.

"I stood there transfixed," Charles was to say. "Just staring while, relentingly, she continued to chat with them.

"She wasn't especially tall," he would remember of his observations as he looked on the three from close by, "but somehow she gave the impression of being both willowy and broad at the same time. She was wearing a loose-fitting, long-sleeved white silk blouse with a collar, and a very tight-fitting plaid skirt. Her hips, though wide, now seemed just right for a body as voluptuous as hers. I still wasn't sure whether I liked the eyes, but I noted that she had exceptionally beautiful white skin, perfect for a blonde. I could literally see it reflecting though the makeup, so clear and tight-pored and flawless—I'd never seen a woman with anything like it before. Her nose, on examining it now, no longer seemed so pugged. I thought, *It's not Lana's nose, but it's a beautiful nose, perfectly in sync with the rest of her features.*

"Most sensuous of all," Charles would tell, "were her lips. I know now these weren't actually as full as they appeared and that she achieved that effect with several shades of lipstick. But my God, such glossy, full lips! She must have been a Rembrandt!

"Not only was hers a beautiful, childlike face," Charles would continue, "but it was a perpetually mobile one, constantly going from one expression to the next. Add to this the animation of her hands and her way of dancing from one foot to the other, and—well, here was a girl who just couldn't stand still!

"I must say," he would add, "that I continued to sense something *heightened* about her as she spoke with these two men. Not that she wasn't smooth as silk—no, she had this act of hers down perfectly. But there was a nervousness about her that wasn't natural. Inwardly, I felt, she lacked poise. She was exaggerated. Sweetly exaggerated. Absolutely captivatingly exaggerated. But exaggerated."

From that thought, Charles Williams' brow would at length unknit until at last he fairly beamed.

"But do you know," he would say, "that in the middle of all those maneuvers as the three of them talked, she took time to look at *me?*!

Yes, right in the middle of that conversation she glanced swiftly across at me—only once, but it was a distinct look that said, 'I'm recognizing you. I know you're still there. And—aha! You finally see who I am, don't you?!'

"Isn't that amazing?!" Charles would ask his listener emphatically.

The rapt listener's answer would probably be a slow swing of the head from side to side in wondering agreement.

"She was aware of my presence," Charles would marvel. "Unmistakably aware, all that time!" And on making this point, Charles might bring his words to an involuntary halt and with his listener silently ponder for an instant the meaning of that scene.

"Well," he would then go on, "There was no place in this world those two guys would rather have been than right there with her! But finally they turned away, letting her go, and came on down the steps. They never once looked at me, you know—never so much as glanced in my direction all this time. It was almost as if they made a point not to look at me. But *she* looked back at me again! My mouth might as well have been hanging open, my expression was one of such awe. She recognized this—and gave me a very warm farewell smile. And then she went inside. I just stood there rooted to the spot, watching the door even after she had gone. I thought, 'I've just seen Marilyn Monroe!'

"A day or two later," he would continue, "I read in the *LA Times* that she'd been at RKO to interview with producers Jerry Wald and Norman Krasna for a part in *Clash by Night*. That proved to be her first costarring role. She was twenty-five years old. It seemed just weeks later that the story of her nude calendar broke, and immediately of course there she was right on the cover of *Life* magazine! In fact, one of the pictures for that story showed her wearing exactly what she had on the day I saw her. And later that year, 20th Century-Fox featured the same outfit in their ads for her first starring vehicle. Remember the slogan? 'Marilyn Monroe—every inch a woman in *Don't Bother to Knock!*'

"Watching those films," Charles was to recall, "not only did I feel I knew her as no one else in the theater did, but I was confirmed in my belief in her talent and even came to love those sensuously down-slanted eyes! Still, I could never shake the impression that she was a little on the frantic side. Exaggerated. Reaching out from somewhere very deep and desperate within.

"Of course I had no idea then," he would say, "that she'd go on to become one of the greatest screen legends of all time. When that happened, and when the past she sprang from became known to the whole world, I felt all the closer to her for realizing she too was truly of the downtrodden and dispossessed. It explained our one small, sweet encounter. Why she'd stayed aware of me when those two studio hotshots came along. Why she'd smiled to me when they left. To me and me only. Charles Williams, the black kid from Wichita!

To that smile Charles, after a second's reflection, would then return with a blissful afterthought:

"You see, she may have given those guys Marilyn Monroe. But she gave me *herself*. She gave me Norma Jeane!"

Notes and Sources

I have been led to *Casting Norma Jeane* by a string of chance interviews which began even as Marilyn Monroe's career soared atop its meteoric trajectory with the filming of *Some Like It Hot*. The exchanges I had, however, were not directly with her. They centered instead around two of her closest relatives—a married couple somewhat past middle age, living modest lives so divorced from the media fanfare surrounding their niece that today one would suppose it to have been humanly impossible.

In that late fall of 1958 through the unique offices of a college friend named Robert Larson, I found myself seated in the living room of Marilyn Monroe's sometime foster mother Enid Knebelkamp, raptly taking in what we now know to be the only interview ever granted to a writer by any of the star's three Atchinson "aunts"—that vital trio of ladies comprised of Mrs Knebelkamp, Marilyn's childhood legal guardian Grace Goddard, and the storied and beloved Aunt Ana Lower. Present with Mrs. Knebelkamp on the one evening we spoke was her husband Sam. In *Casting Norma Jeane* this pair appears along with all of the twenty-year-old starlet's other closest relatives in my chapter entitled "Scroll of Life."

During several subsequent months in 1958 and 1959, I also had three lengthy interviews with Enid Knebelkamp's close neighbor and trusted friend, who was indeed my colleague Robert Larson's mother, the sophisticated and discerning Catherine Larson. Mrs. Larson joins Mrs. Knebelkamp in my chapter called "Artichoke Queen."

Not least, on innumerable occasions between the fall of 1958 and the spring of 1963, I interviewed Robert Larson himself (who happened once to have been the successful child movie actor billed in his heyday as *Bobby* Larson). Mr. Larson never met Marilyn Monroe, but at home he had always taken a lively, bemused, and wondering interest in everything his mother had to say about her, which he now repeated to me as one thoroughly under the famed actress's spell.

In connection with these four sources—Enid and Sam Knebelkamp, Catherine Larson, and Robert Larson—I use the word "interview." Alas, as the saying goes, life is what happens while you're making other plans. My great ambition, then, as a budding film auteur of nineteen, was to write *for* Marilyn Monroe, not *about* her. It hardly crossed my mind to take any but the most incidental and cursory notes of the fascinating things these invaluable witnesses told me. Therefore, although it seems to me that almost every anecdote I heard from them has remained in my memory word for word to this day, in the absence of conventional documentation my rule throughout *Casting Norma Jeane* has been to rely strictly on other firsthand sources for any actual speech appearing between quotation marks in the text, as hereinbelow noted. In this regard I am particularly indebted to Berniece Miracle and Mona Rae Miracle, whose indispensable *My Sister Marilyn: A Memoir of Marilyn Monroe* preserves the sequence in which words were spoken on four different occasions that figured importantly in the story as it was passed on to me.

Of course no story in the world ever suffered less than this one did from a scarcity of source material. The bibliography that follows represents only a tiny fraction of the veritable library of Marilyn Monroe research, biography and memoir that has arisen over the past half century—an accumulation as remarkable as anything of its kind in existence. From this repository, to be sure, works bearing upon the late summer and early fall of 1946 have provided *Casting Norma Jeane* with a wealth of factual corroboration, descriptive detail and chronological context, as additionally cited below. Nonetheless I must say that I owe the kernel and thrust of almost every scene in this book rather to the accounts of the four uniquely placed witnesses whom I have named. *J.G.*

1. **Planes and Angles**, Pages 1-3.
   "*What can I do for you?* et al.: Guiles/Norma Jean, 69-70.
   "*You can tell with some faces*: Parsons, 172.
   See also: Gilmore, 86. Guiles/Legend, 99. Spoto, 110.
2. **Looking Glass**, Pages 5-14.
   "*What the hell is that?* et al.: Crown, 31.
   "*We can't photograph her that way*, et al: Spoto, 110, 119.
   See also: Wolfe, 184. Zolotow, 57.

3. **Particles of Light**, Pages 15-23.

"*All I want you to do is to come in that door*, et al.: Carpozi, 21-2.

"*I just want you to project yourself*: Parsons/ Tell It To Louella, 172-3.

"*Action*!:Zolotow, 59-60

See also: Barris, 61-3. Goodman, 230. Guiles/ Legend, 100. Guiles/Norma Jean, 71. Morgan/Undisclosed, 66. Spoto, 111. Victor, 263. Warren, 95, 99-100.

4. **Ford Sports Coupe**, Pages 25-36.

"*Why did you cut off my allowance?* et al.: Spoto 108.

"*Well gee, Norma Jeane*, et al.: Dougherty/To Norma Jeane, 131-135.

"*Your suit doesn't fit*, et al.: Dougherty/Secret Happiness, 99-103.

See also: Guiles/Legend, 102-3.

5. **Oceans of Print**, Pages 37-42.

"*I've got it*: Zolotow, 18, 61-2.

"*Finest studio in the world*, et al.: Monroe/ Hecht, 15, 53-4.

"I told you!: Wolfe 189.

See also: Miracle, 8. Spoto, 251. Morgan/
Confidential, 32. Victor, 123.

6. **Five O'Clock Girls**, Pages 43-47.

"Jet, this is Norma Jeane, et al.: Author's
interview of Jet Fore, April 29, 1989.

See also: Mosley, 176. Zolotow, 1.

7. **Broken Cobwebs**, Pages 49-55.

"Aunt Norma Jeane, your hair is blond *now*:
Miracle, 12, 17-8, 65-66.

8. **Hypnotist's Watch**, Pages 57-65.

"That's so ridiculous, et al.: Miracle, 67-69.

See also: Spoto, 10-11. Zolotow, 69.

9. **House of Monroe**, Pages 67-77.

"The aura of a trip in a time machine, et al.:
Miracle, 12, 53, 73-74, 86-88.

"Wanderlust charm: Gilmore, 29-32.

"Neat as a pin: Spoto, 2-4.

See also: Monroe/Hecht, 54.

10. **Carole Lind**, Pages 79-82.

*"The casting directors want me to change my
name*, et al.: Author's interview of Jet Fore,

April 29, 1989.

See also: Miracle 53. Monroe/Hecht 54.

Summers, 31. Victor, 212.

11. **Sacred Space**, Pages 83-87.

"Marilyn. That's a nice first name, et al.:
Monroe/Hecht 53-4.

"That sounds real pretty: Zolotow, 62.

"Why not use Monroe? et al.: Barris, 63-4.

"Someday it'll be you *putting your handprints*:
Gilmore, 55-6.

See also: Zolotow, 18-19.

12. **Cat and Mouse**, Pages 89-99.

"Hurry up or we'll be late, et al.: Miracle,
37, 78-80.

See also: Victor, 212.

13. **Celluloid Kingdom**, Pages 101-112.

"She's pretty and sweet and soft: Miracle,
3, 36-7, 80-85.

14. **Smoke in the Wind**, Pages 113-120.

"But please, Jimmie, sign the papers: Dougherty/
Secret Happiness, 28-30, 101-6.

"Finally, as it got darker I felt myself sigh:
Dougherty/To Norma Jeane, 31-2, 55,
126, 135-7, 139-40, 145-6.

See also: Guiles/Norma Jean, 41. Guiles/
Legend, 102-3. Morgan/Undisclosed, 48.
Spoto, 75. Zolotow, 43.

15. **Black Lace**, Pages 121-134.

"But André, I don't want to get mm-mm-married,
et al.: de Dienes 13, 16-78.

See also: Goodman, 224. Mailer, 54-8.
Morgan/Undisclosed, 60-1.
Summers, 17-8.

16. **Scroll of Life**, Pages 135-148.

"I'm a free woman! et al.: Miracle, 90-1.

See also: Hoyt, 24. Morgan/Confidential, 32.
Zolotow, 18-19.

17. **Arcing Wave**, Pages 149-156.

"She seemed awestruck by the very notion, et al.:
Dougherty/Secret Happiness, 106-8.

"What'll they be calling you? et al.: Dougherty/
To Norma Jeane, 144, 153-4.

18. **Mimosa Blossoms**, Pages 157-163.
   "I have something on my m-m-mind, et al.:
      Miracle, 91-2.

19. **Voice from Olympus**, Pages165-174.
   "Please, could I keep my mother's maiden name?:
      Martin, 38.
   "All right, Monroe's *in*: Carpozi, 22.
   "You are to me a Marilyn: Guiles/Legend, 100.
   "It's got a nicer flow—with the two M's:
      Summers, 30-1.
   "Say it, et al.: Spoto, 114-5.
   See also: Gilmore, 87.
      Morgan/Undisclosed, 66.

20. **Parade of the Stars**, Pages 175-203.
   "This is the end of Norma Jeane: Monroe/
      Hecht, 31, 55.
   "You're going to be a great *movie star*:
      Zolotow, 18.
   "How do you spell Marilyn?: Martin, 38.
   See also: Belmont, 14. Cunningham, 35.
      Dougherty/To Norma Jeane, 10.
      Gilmore, 39, 49, 55, 63-4, 196.

Guiles/Norma Jean, 21. *Los Angeles Times,* November 23, 1946. Martin, 38. Miracle, 19, 32, 46, 68-9, 74. Monroe/Hecht,   11-14.   Morgan/Undisclosed, 19, 66-67. Spoto, 11, 19, 31-3, 39. Victor, 104, 212. Wolfe, 17, 116. Zolotow,18-9.

21. **Artichoke Queen,** Pages 205-213.

"*As I came up Enid's front walk,* et al.: Author's interview of Catherine Larson, March 29, 1959.

See also: Glaeg, letter February 19, 1963. Morgan/Confidential, 99.

22. **Blonde of the Day,** Pages 215-225.

"*I was strolling down Gower Avenue,* et al.: Author's interview of Charles Williams, August 5, 1991.

Back cover.

"*She started out with less than any girl I ever knew*: Victor, 279

Bibliography

Barris, George. *Marilyn: Her Life in her Own Words*. Citadel Press, 2003.

Belmont, Georges. *Marilyn Monroe and the Camera*. Little, Brown and Company, 1989.

Carpozi Jr, George. *Marilyn Monroe: Her Own Story*. Universal-Award House, 1973.

Crown, Lawrence. *Marilyn at Twentieth Century Fox*. Planet Books,1987.

Cunningham, Ernest W. *The Ultimate Marilyn*. Renaissance Books, 1998.

deDienes, André. *Marilyn Mon Amour*. Bracken Books, 1993.

Dougherty, James E. *The Secret Happiness of Marilyn Monroe*. Playboy Press, 1976.

Dougherty, James. *To Norma Jeane with Love, Jimmie*. BeachHouse Books, 2001.

Gilmore, John. *Inside Marilyn Monroe*. Ferine Books, 2007.

Glaeg, James. Letter to Maurice Zolotow, February 19, 1963. Maurice Zolotow Archives, Harry Ransom Humanities Research Center, University of Texas at Austin.

Goodman, Ezra. *The Fifty Year Decline and Fall of Hollywood*. MacFadden Books, 1962.

Guiles, Fred Lawrence. *Legend: The Life and Death of Marilyn Monroe*. Stein and Day, 1984.

Guiles, Fred Lawrence. *Norma Jean: The Life of Marilyn Monroe*. MacGraw-Hill Book Company, 1969.

Hoyt, Edwin P. *Marilyn: The Tragic Venus*. Duell, Sloan and Pearce, 1965.

Mailer, Norman. *Marilyn: A Biography*. Grosset& Dunlap, Inc., 1973.

Martin, Pete. *Will Acting Spoil Marilyn Monroe?* Pocket Books, Inc., 1956.

Miracle, Berniece Baker, and Miracle, Mona Rae. *My Sister Marilyn: A Memoir of Marilyn Monroe*. Algonquin Books of Chapel Hill, 1994.

Monroe, Marilyn, with Hecht, Ben. *My Story*. Stein and Day, 1976.

Morgan, Michelle. *Marilyn Monroe: Private and Confidential*. Skyhorse Publishing, 2012.

Morgan, Michelle. *Marilyn Monroe: Private and Undisclosed*. Carroll & Graf Publishers, 2007.

Mosley, Leonard. *Zanuck: The Rise and Fall of Hollywood's Last Tycoon*. Little, Brown and Company, 1984.

Parsons, Louella. *Tell It To Louella*. Lancer Books, 1963.

"Santa Claus Lane Opens With Parade of Stars,"
Los Angeles Times, November 23, 1946.

Spoto, Donald. *Marilyn Monroe: The Biography.*
Cooper Square Press, 1993.

Summers, Anthony. *Goddess: The Secret Lives
of Marilyn Monroe.* New American Library,
1986.

Victor, Adam. *The Marilyn Encyclopedia.* The
Overlook Press, 1999.

Warren, Doug, *Betty Grable: The Reluctant Movie
Queen.* St Martin's Press, 1981.

Wasson, George. 20th Century-Fox interoffice
memo from Legal Department to Harry
Brand, Publicity Department, December
8, 1946. Reproduced on Swann Auction
Galleries website at www.swanngalleries.com.

Wolfe, Donald H. *The Last Days of Marilyn
Monroe.* William Morrow and Company,
Inc., 1998.

Zolotow, Maurice. *Marilyn Monroe.* Harper &
Row, Publishers, Inc., 1990.

2319301R00123

Printed in Great Britain
by Amazon.co.uk, Ltd.,
Marston Gate.